GW01458182

# MAYS
## 17

V
Varsity Publications

Varsity Publications Ltd
Old Examination Hall
Free School Lane
Cambridge CB2 3RF

First published 2009 by Varsity Publications Ltd

Copyright © 2009 Varsity Publications Ltd

ISBN 978-0-902240-39-1

Typeset in Caslon.
Cover colour is PANTONE® Blue 072 M.
Printed and bound by Y Lolfa Cyf. in Talybont, Wales

Original concept by Peter Ho Davies, Adrian Woolfson, Ron Dimant

British Library Cataloguing in Publication Data.
A CIP catalogue record of this book is available from the British Library.

Further copies of this book and other titles in the series can be bought through most booksellers or direct from Varsity Publications at the address above or at:
*www.varsity.co.uk/themays*

# Guest Editor
## *Patti Smith*

We are indebted to our College sponsors:

## *Cambridge*

Churchill College, Fitzwilliam College, Gonville & Caius College, Homerton College, Jesus College, Lucy Cavendish College, Newnham College, Pembroke College, Queens' College, Sidney Sussex College, Trinity College, Trinity Hall

## *Oxford*

Christ Church, Corpus Christi College, Jesus College, Merton College, New College, Oriel College, St Hugh's College, St John's College, Trinity College, University College, Wadham College

# Mays 17

| | |
|---:|:---|
| *Guest Editor* | Patti Smith |
| *Editors* | Peter Morelli and Decca Muldowney |
| *Managing Editor* | Michael Derringer |
| *Oxford Associate Editor* | Christopher Morley |
| *Poetry Committee* | Tom Gilliver, Ned Hercock, Dan Hitchens, Ewan Jones, Annie Katchinska, Ailsa McDermid, Lorenzo Mesfut, Edward Rice, Charlotte Runcie, Vicky Sparrow |
| *Prose Committee* | Daisy Belfield, Patrick Kingsley, Clementine Stott, Sebastian Gertz, Maartje Geussens, Francis Winfield |
| *Art Committee* | Jane Issler Hall, Francesca Perry |
| *Cover Design* | Anna Trench |
| *Copy Editors* | Izzy Finkel, Colm Flanagan, Hugo Gye |
| *With thanks to* | Emma Hogan |

# Poetry

# Photography and Art

# Prose

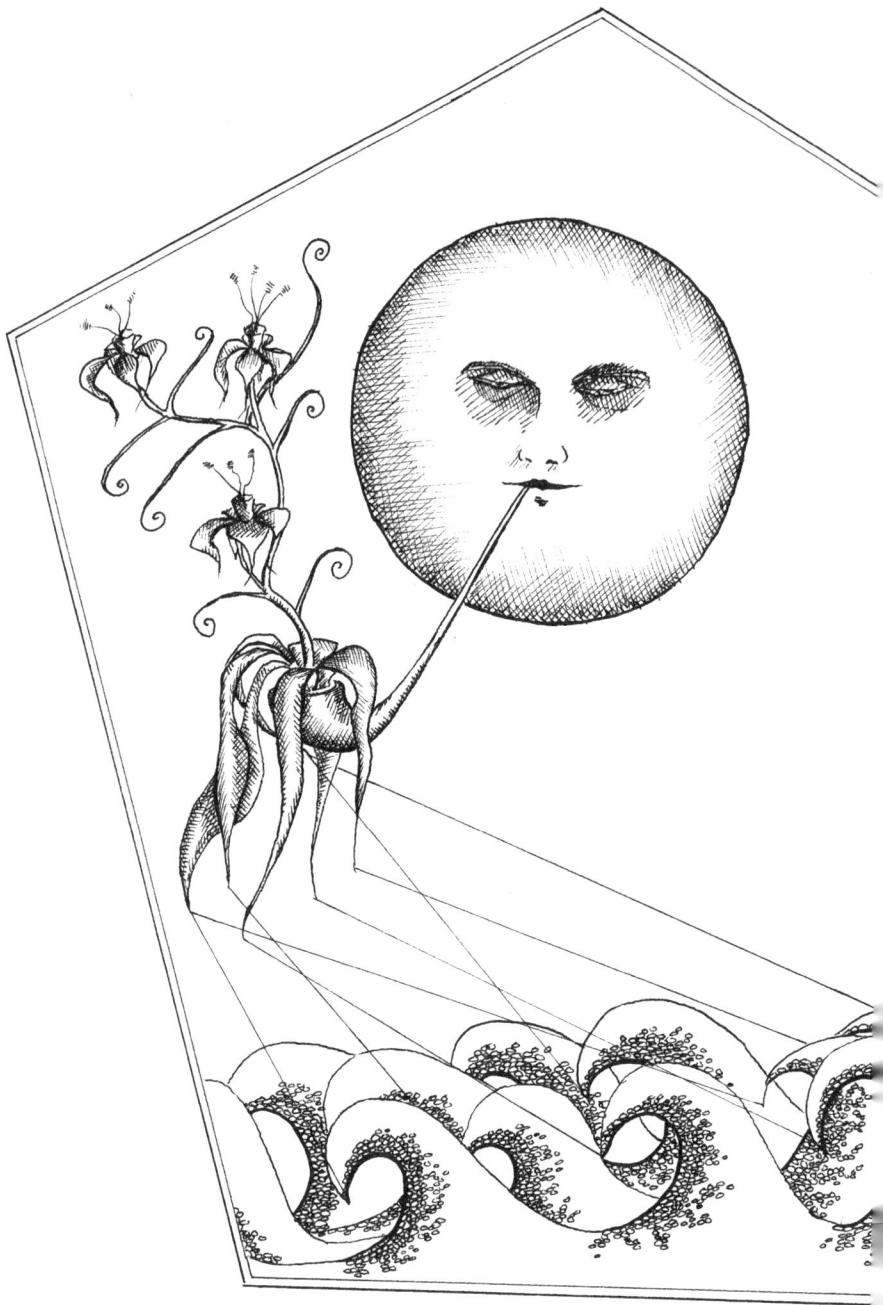

# Poetry

# A few words
## *Patti Smith*

When I was asked to make a selection of poems for *Mays 17*, I had first to search within myself. Who am I to judge the work of another poet? How could I best serve? I finally decided not to judge but to arrange certain poems that somehow complemented one other, so as to offer a diverse yet interrelated body of work.

This concept gave me the freedom to choose a few poems that I didn't prefer, yet stayed with me, and had particular technical merit. Others I chose for lyric beauty, clarity, wit or a unique sense of self-containment. I feel all of the poems here stand on their own and yet sit well with the ones surrounding them. I also considered the visual aesthetic of the poems and how each could be best presented on the page.

I had a notion that some of the poems were the result of assignments, as there was a repetition of concepts and certain word use. I chose poems that seemed to shed the weight of any specific task, thus transcending it.

In the passing days I have found that some of the poems that I did not choose have also stayed with me. I feel confident in this selection but I believe every poem presented had merit. So I take this opportunity to salute all the poets. In the end, if one is meant to be a poet so shall one be, whether recognized or not.

Poets' labours are often unsung, so let us now enjoy a bit of music, through the pages of the *Mays 17*, thus heralding the future.

# Blow Blue Wind
## *Alashiya Gordes*

Blow, blue wind, the tent will fly,
And I, weak part, will sunder.
Fever-blown and eyes run out
And wishes washing over.

Whispers grow and thoughts fall snow,
I rise and break beyond me.
Open sky and roll on rocks;
The clouds bell loud and cradle rocks.

# MORO

## Charlotte Geater

There was a bowl on your windowsill.
At first I thought you'd left them there too long
and that oranges could burn, like me last summer,
elbows caught out by the sun.

The flesh was purple. We swapped bruises,
comments on the news. Our bank accounts
were knee-deep in red. You listed locations, and all
I could think (*Belfast*) (*Seattle*) was

this orange is from another country (*Italy*).
Your fingers were too pink for March, each tip
like a thimble. There were charms falling

at your neck, and I, dainty and unsure
leaned over the bin and spat out three seeds
at empty wicker, like gristle, gristle, bone.

# The Seven of Us
*Molly Stern*

The seven of us
had guns in our lungs when we sang to her
squeezed into her throat
she was deep like an excavation.
our pet mouse had escaped my pocket & was asleep in her liver
and she said her stomach felt like a little toad.
we said maybe the mouse is in your liver
but she never took us seriously.

We told her the soup was blessed
that's why it tasted like that. that was what we told her.
we had five sausages gripped in our hands
and she was below in her raincoat.
she had scrubbed the oven substantially
even though we disagreed with her methods.
she laughed. what a multi-faceted amphibian she was!
we contained ourselves, her duck-with-blue-cheese
threatened us as it lay on our chests.

Yesterday I wrote her a poem
it was about the bag of blueberries
kevin had sat on.
it was erotic.
I recited it a few times while she made flan.
dreck! she pronounced.
her flan gleamed and leapt.
I eyed it and suggested fewer eggs.

The seven of us
imagined her far away in a glass café
knitting facial hair on a bed of eight wondrous berries
the way a mouse feels cushioned in the heart
he is bursting with juice, with air in his bones
his ears are creaking with the weight
of a thousand bees.

When I thought of us
I laughed in a way which was both like eating a melon and giving
up on life.

She had emerged from our mud pit glowing
and we had prized her the way a mouse does.
we nested in her, made her collarbone our roof
used all the little knuckles and bones
cried into her esophagus, spread our crockery in her pelvis.
and when she laughed we trembled.

# Orison

*Johnny Regan*

I am the author of the parkway's bleached interstice.
I wrote the line on the dark desperate orison,
the one about the exchange of grit, rubber and light,
the commerce of cynosure: the border of
the car door effaced, that desperate horizon.
"I've lived in Maryland for years and I don't, I
don't – roll down the window, I don't want——."
Easing and gliding now: ten pounds of red meat
the tumescence in and under me, gliding all the
same. Can the car door abrogate the tumor? Can the
prayer of the road's border allow me to pass
over space like the dying sun's fulmination?
Shit that weeping light's scary can you turn it off.

# lessons on garden trees (i)

*marcelle olivier*

never dig beneath a ficus tree:
the soil there is milky, and moist,
and you will find only the spineless
larvae of insect heavies.

never dig beneath a ficus tree:
the roots are hard as iron, thick
as their lives have been long,
and remorseless to shovels and saws.

never dig beneath a ficus tree:
there are secrets there.
not gold, not silver, not amethyst stones;

but – always – the dark formless
treasure of roped and selfish bones.

# The Winter Empress

*Laura Marsh*

No need to pause on a stalactite. Beaming
she showed everyone an athlete caught mid
high jump, embarrassed the private screams
of big-eared bats with glowing eyes. She slid

in with the rain. Colours dripped from her cheeks,
made the room pink and our hair flyaway,
shocked into the coronets of chic
girls drowning, fanning haywire. She came to stay

like a replacement for silk. Thin ice.
The allure of china and fur coats we trust,
forgetting, hooked on the hopeless goodbyes
that replay, attracted with the charge of dust.

We hold hands and crackle. It is never night,
only snowy static, the persistent thought
frosting over everything. In her light
we flicker, change channels, always dawn.

# The Imitation of Christ

*Michael Trafford*

The fine, fond, fleshly tapir knows
The problems that the hippos pose
To pass the time

Will not perturb his think, which goes
On thinking, 'hind his mobile nose,
In realms sublime.

# Jack
## *Emily Tesh*

One autumn I romanced the winter painter.
He said he'd thought of branching out, of red,
put his mouth into my hair and cried

icicles. November drew a fainter
gasp from him: go on, you fool, I said,
when he was lingering. And I'm deprived

these days, of colour: my hair bears the taint
of winter's breath, snow-grey; in my dark bed
the memory of ice-melt sweat survives,

his fingerprints that melted on me wait –
so I sleep on the window seat instead
of sinking into frost again. I lied,

you know. All this was his idea, this farce.
Sometimes he paints me love-notes on the glass.

# Incident
## *Ailsa McDermid*

Antiseptic acridity and the paper-plastic rip of plaster cases
were my solace, if not hers, as we wiped and soothed and bandaged.
Charity so physical it was biblical in its application.

I traced mental networks back, constructed parallels,
the tumble from the bike, the smell of cut knees,
kissed and plastered up on the stool in the kitchen.

Then next week, concentrating my way home,
my mind turned off down an unlit road
and there it all was, inescapably was,
the woman in the gutter, hair tangled in the bike's metal,
screams, bike chain gouges in bloody side, the end,
more blackness, social networks behind drawn curtains.

We'd chatted over the teapot that afternoon,
agreed that a normal life was the one to lead,
but what network for her to reconstruct that rape,
fashioned by her deconstructed world as
incident, nothing more?

# Futterneid

## *Richard O'Brien*

Your plate glares up at me. The table
turns to drink and so do I, mocked
by the chosen octopus, and now unable

to contain the envy which unlocks
and raids the fridges of my brain,
making a midnight feast.          Hey, look,

a pickled heart, a liver pumped to drain.
It's bitter over here. He's big on peanut butter;
otherwise, it's standard, in the main –

a few aberrant tastes, but most vanilla, not a
one you'd not spit out in trusting company,
and nothing much you couldn't cookie-cutter.

Best served cold, or left fermenting gradually,
the older stock might turn to vinegar, or just
dry up like Durex in a wallet – but generally

what's bottled up can stay that way.        You call it lust;
I call it *futterneid*. It's nothing hard to hide;
I usually get by without all that much fuss,

and so do you. You've still got room inside;
pick up your fork. Your food is getting cold,
and I forgot to bring a scarf. Alright, I lied,

I chose to go without. It made the night hold
onto me with sharper contours. *Futterneid*,
two sins combined, a knife that scrapes the soul,

your neighbour's plate, if you can make so bold.
Your body is a problem that cannot be solved.

.

# Grey Skies
## *Colette Sensier*

Outside the house,
on a silk of skinny acorns
bold lilies throw off leaves
as a man throws off his jacket,
we lie making a circle on the grass,
on berries and their silent, holy
curvature. We show them
something utterly unlike
themselves.

A dark,
pungent flower
disassociates, the fading smell,
as blue rivers pull away from the land
like men going about their lives – hearing the sound
of the sea.

# come with me
## *(i thought you knew i did not love you*
## *when i said* come with me*)*

# *marcelle olivier*

the ebony grove was a good place:
the grass was flattened but still green
 – elephants had been there that morning,
waiting out the first part of the day in
the familiar shade of the trees, touching
trunks with trunks for the smell of previous
visitors; i have often seen them do likewise
in the thicket of palms by the crescent-shaped dambo –
and there was a place where the sun
fell through the leaves like bits of rainbow.

it was not far to walk, but the impenetrable
afternoon heat kept everyone lounging
in the boma reading second-hand paperbacks,
and the animals would only move again at dusk;
if the grove was empty it would stay so
until the hippos in the oxbow began bleating.

you took off your wedding ring. i watched
as you found a place for it: a ledge on a small
anthill covered with butterflies. they made
a brief, colourful protest before settling
down to resume the search for moisture,
and one sat for a long time on my hand probing

for sweat, blinking its wings. you eventually
lost your patience with both of us.

i saw the unexpected above me: an old beehive,
three nests woven into one, and a lizard disguised as a twig.
i may have seen a bright green diamond-headed snake,
slipping like a rod of hot glass through the branches
without making a sound. then again, i may not have:
it was hard to concentrate on anything but the heat.
i imagined myself there, i imagined myself in love.

however soft the grass was, it was hard. you said
you loved that sound, but i could tell you were hurt.
i learnt while watching you dress me
that the ebony grove was a good place to break hearts;
amidst the scatter of light, seeds, and dried-up shit.

# The Bishop Confesses

*Tiffany Bergin*

All day long I smell their funerals
and sit among their secrets
hearing sounds I can't decipher.
Their souls sing off-key when we are alone.
I listen to their stories
in the seclusion only the dead know.
I kneel beside their ghosts.
When winter comes to this wooden chapel,
I press my flesh against the floorboards
and feel the coldness of their bones.
They tell me what it is to be invisible,
when the stillness of the world is too much to bear.
I tell them I have said too much about salvation
and too little of fear

# Submarine
## *Ashley Riches*

On lighter air they circle, bold
And close to where I swim. They dance
Off (I reach). Then, spreading by untold holes
In the suspension, they flick on

(Sad I don't see them go) below
Amongst the reef. Beneath the lap
Slap flounder of the surface, shoals
Glint, glimmer, hovering. Perhaps

Through coral towers their bodies move,
Wreathe glittering flowers and flashes, mark
As one the speech that might seem love.
It cannot reach the quiet dark.

Here echoes and re-echoes, silence
Salt and sand and fish like jilted
Toys fall, jetsam round the defenceless
Wreck, a metal hulk and silt.

# Carpe Diem, or What You Can Learn From Fish

*John Syfret*

In the Abbey garden
the carp lie dark
in pools of sly green.
Patient, stiller than the Linden
or squeezing and slipping
lazily easily.
So should I,
and also nibble the toes
of unwary paddlers.

# Anvers
## *Edward Maltby*

You blink through the barriers
To staccato youths with square-stacked fists,
Who roll, Marlboro, Marlboro, Marlboro

Tati, Quick!

On the metro steps a woman gargles and sobs,
Slavers chewed-up words in drops

Folle

Old men push rattling coughs
Spit balled gobs to rivet the street
On a black drum top roast burst brown knots

Marrons

Eyes wide, hot, he, stabs a dazzling glare

Voyou

The escalator folds the crowd past empty drunks who with
Tick-tock hands shift a mass of print, sloughing tons

At the platform, stop.
Morning shift gathers
Old hands on watch fobs

Lovers' grey breath hovers
Crossed girders chop
Step
Bright clock winks dots
"00"

And with a heavenly crack like the breaking of a seal,
the train, the metro most modern arcs upwards out of Anvers
projecting forwards like a hilltop statue's gaze
pitching forwards like a picket's white-knuckled hope like a second
chance, like your tongue when you choke, like a second chance
pitched forwards like the angel who can't close his wings
and under each other's weight we all pile in

and there's a rumble in our chests as the engine begins
and though I know, in this press of breath and eyes,
where through the carriage window I can see the sun rise
though I know that at Jaurès it'll drop down into the earth
and the wheels we feel beneath our feet will only take us to work,

still while the carriage twists above the city as it stirs
it's like a switch has been thrown, the line misremembered
like we're flying through a different dawn
or come untethered from the day

"Too Sick-making"

# Photography

# Lizzie Robinson

Dylan
Spencer-Davidson

# Miguel Santa Clara

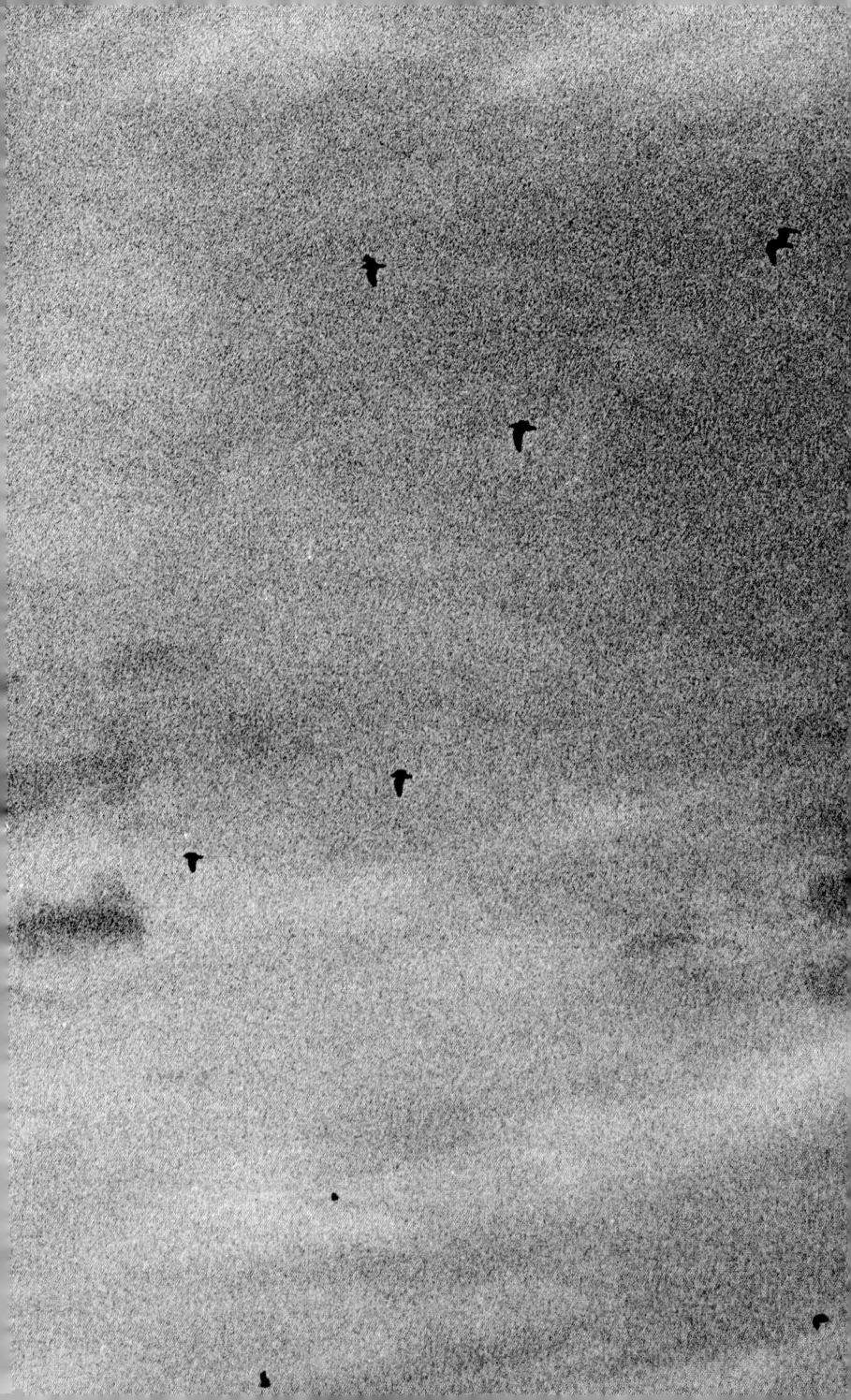

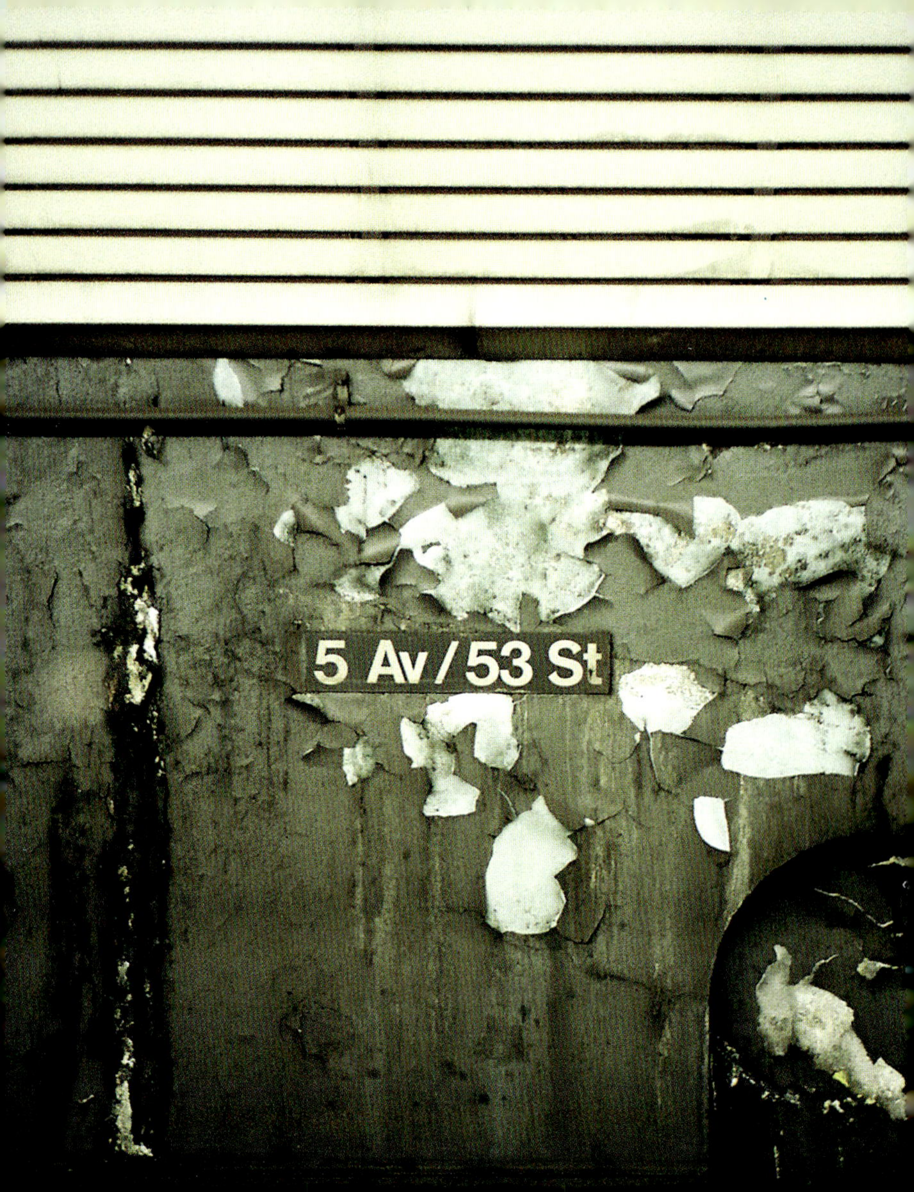
5 Av / 53 St

# Francesca Perry

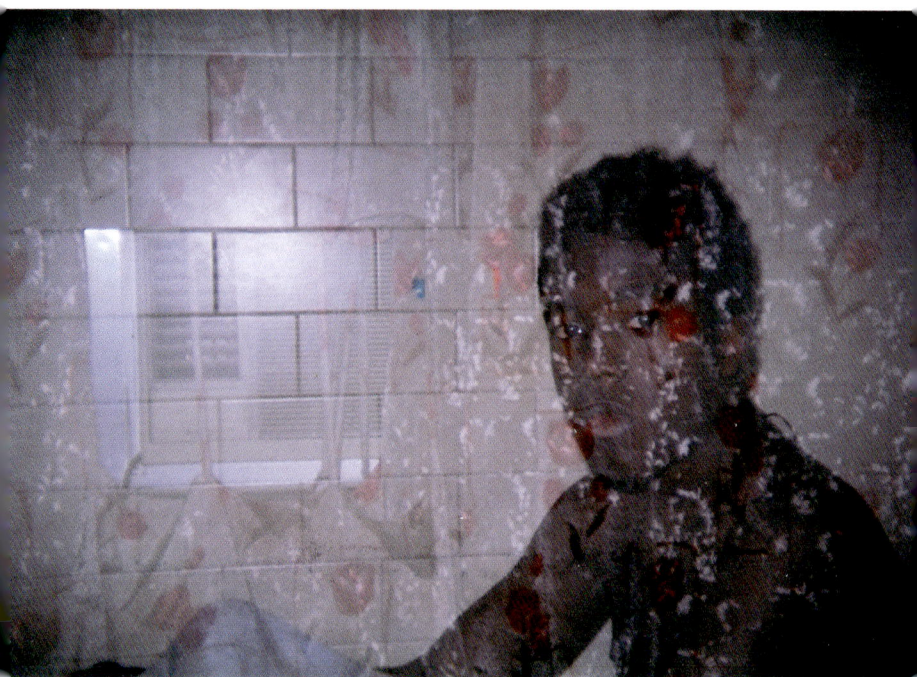

# Adam Hines-Green

Patrick Kingsley

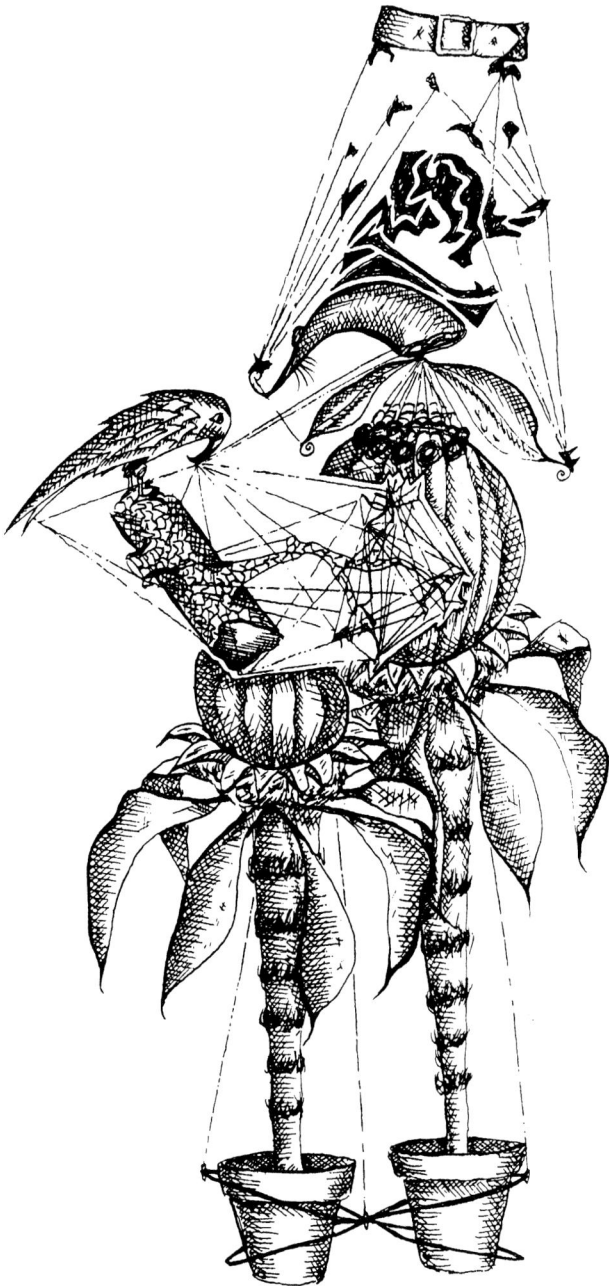

# Prose

# A Rough Guide to Time Travel

*Jesse Bordwin*

*AN INTRODUCTION or ON LOSS*

H ello. I would like you to imagine this scene. You are walking down the street, the main street of your hometown. Maybe it's called Main Street, but maybe it's called Broad Street. Or possibly something more inspired. Or just Church Street. Perhaps it actually ends in the town's church. Or begins. There are children with ice-cream and old men on benches with newspapers. This is an America. Suddenly, behind you, a squeal of tires. A woman screams. You turn and you see your husband lying immobile on the ground a couple of feet in front of a car that has one tire up on the curb. It could be your daughter. Or your mother. Your lover, and nobody knew you were together. This doesn't matter. This guide is not interested in being constrained by the circumstantial. The two objects, the car and the person, or even a dog, seem not to have anything to do with one another. When you see them, they are two separate and distinct objects in time. It is only later that you realize what they have to do with one another. And by that time, by the time that causality reaches actuality, it's too late. Your grandfather is dead, crushed by a stray cinderblock, and your son, your only son, is shot in the head. Three times.[1]   And you have, without portent or precedent, lost, just as I have, just as we all have.

---

1. The second two were gratuitous.  Nobody ever figured out what they meant.

Suddenly you realize that we are all guilty, all of us, because we are the living. When we weigh produce and ignore postcards and when we get scared of bathtubs, we have made it past the dead, like runners in a lethal race. More explicitly, I like to think of a miniature racetrack, like one you might see when they race greyhounds. Except there are bunnies lining the gate. One of their names is Donovan and another is Miss Anastasia the Proud. They start off hopping along the track, but are soon set upon by disease, booby traps, and random acts of violence from their human handlers. The racing bunnies who escape keep going, because it's what they do, but every time they survive another lap, they have to hop over the disemboweled remains (which in more romantic flights I call *viscera*) of their fallen comrades. It is possible these rabbits might be too dumb to think about it, but they are the guilty ones.

We, on the other hand, experience and understand these feelings. Return to Main Street. You run over to the body of your son. Who was just recovering from impetigo. Or something. There is shock, certainly, shock is necessary. Disbelief. And sadness, yes. But oh, the guilt. It comes at the first silence, whether on the way to the hospital, in the back of the ambulance, waiting in that sterile room with art reproductions on the walls, or maybe it doesn't come until months later, when the friends finally stop bringing over cold chicken parmesan for you to reheat and your father has flown back down to Florida because you said you no longer need the company at night. In that first moment where you have the time to yourself, you'll get hit with a flood of regret.

There are five questions that, more than any others, we find our clients asking themselves:

1. Why couldn't I have been [insert tragedy here. for example: mauled by that deranged circus monkey] instead of [insert loved one here. for example: my betrothed, Matsaharu Yasaitaku]?

2. Did I see it coming?[2]

3. What happened, and what was the exact time that it happened?[3]

4. Why didn't I love him/her/it harder/better/stronger/more?

5. Could I have done something to change it?

Let's start over. Or change pace. I feel claustrophobic. Or overburdened.

*A CHANGE OF PACE:*
*HOW TO BE A CHRONONAUT AND NOT A*
*CHRONONAUGHT*

The first things you should always remember are your **ECT**s:

---

2. People look for patterns. They get messages from the arrangements of cars in a parking lot or freckles on their mistress's back. The long trail of evidence leading up to a divorce, the aggressive letters and the slammed doors, stretch before and after the length of the relationship, forming a greater design than two people ever could. One man became obsessed with decoding and recoding the world around him until he discovered the very substance of time itself, the rules and regulations, the anomalies and footnotes. His name was Professor Saul Wyle, and he founded this company before starving himself to death when he refused to get off a carnival ride. Some say that for days after his death the ride went round and round, playing the tinny music in repetitive vertigo, and people swore that the movement was his and not that of the plastic pony between his legs.

3. These days, so many of us crave that specificity of tragedy. I was only a small child when the Towers of the World Trade Center in the city of New York (by the temple of music and near the fountain of light) came tumbling to the ground. My very first thought was that they were getting swallowed by a black hole: so much mass in such a tightly perfect city imploding into such a small space. I then spent the next hour fixed to the television, looking at the small dial in the middle of my watch thinking, "Everyone my parents' age remembers where they were and what day it was when President Kennedy was shot (which was, not incidentally, the same day I was to be born on, decades later). I have to remember, for my children, and their potential children, that today is September the eleventh. The eleventh of September." I repeated it to myself over and over again. It was much later that I realized how much of my emotional capacity was wasted that day, memorizing that date, when people started calling this event in space and time "Nine-Eleven." Nobody could ever forget. I was born at 9:45 in the morning, but I think about all the little children waiting to be born, one every twelve seconds. Which means that every day, ten children will be nine-eleven children. And when the obstetrician calls the time, the mother's brow will furrow and the father will sigh. Some fictionally-appropriate aunt will tisk when the news gets back to her: "Ah, the baby will never make it far in life. Whenever they try to rise, they will fall." At ten a day, seventy a week, and three thousand, six hundred and forty a year (subtracting six that will die of malnutrition in Africa, one of malpractice in Uruguay, one in a mudslide in Laos, and one that was even secretly euthanized in a small, Kansas hospital by the father because the child was born on 13:13, military time, September the Eleventh itself), soon there will be an army of disenfranchised, disillusioned babies born under the shadow of the two towers. They will, one day, find each other, through the channels and sluice-gates of the internet and be drawn magnetically to one another in diners and cafes around the world, and together they'll come to our headquarters, demanding to leap backward in time, to stop the catastrophe that stamped them with ineptitude and stole from them their successes. We are taking measures to prepare for this event, with snipers, trapeze artists, and other security precautions in the works. You are, I promise, safe in our hands.

ECTs
Chrono-Objectivity.
The Ghost of Christmas Past
Specificity of Experience

**ECT**s. We say it again because of its importance. See below for more.

**Chrono-Objectivity**. It means that everything that has ever happened, every event in time and time itself, has no truth or moral value. All of our research points towards this. A father, at times soft and gentle and at others harsh and cruel, beats his ripe, brown daughter in some dark backwater in time. One of her eyes seems to barely cling to its root. Oh, you say, this is bad, this thing is, in itself, a bad thing. It's true, no doubt, that the father is a bad man. His intent is cruel and his blows are hard. But imagine, once again if you will, an alien observer privy to the scene. Her name, translated, is Daphne Fissure. She watches, but has no concept that the striking causes pain, no sense of the relationship between the two. She cannot understand scars, or the persistence of hurt. She just sees two ladles of flesh in a given space, touching sometimes, sometimes not. This is the lens of time. And possibly, in this way, all acts that fit into the forward rolling of time are good acts. Maybe what we do is the only 'bad event' possible. We are disrupters... we are criminal. We'll revisit this.

**The Ghost of Christmas Past**. There was a book I read a long time ago called A Christmas Carol.[4] I want you to think of the ghosts. Or perhaps, in a way, you are the Scrooge and the Ghosts of Christmases Past. You are the wallpaper on walls. You are the air the memories of past peoples breathe, or, more accurately, the infinite number of places they choose not to occupy. You can touch them, but they can-

---

4. We've recently begun including excerpts in the supplemental materials packet.

not feel you. To understand this is imperative.[5] Another way to think of it: you are the Ghosts of Christmases Yet to Come, except in the past. What we will never be, what no one will ever be is the Ghost of Christmas that Could Have Been. Another way to think of it: don't even consider the existence of the Specter of Holidays That Were Yet To Be. That If Only This Had Happened. Another way to think of it: absorb, absorption. These are, of course, different aspects of the same word. But the letters change, drastically.[6] Say this ten times fast: Contiguous continuity, continuous contiguity.

**Specificity of Experience.** Standing on a street corner on the Lower West Side, you might hear a tall man dressed in all black except for a bright red tie shout something like: "We are trapped in our own heads, in our own bodies, and the closest we can get to each other is by rubbing our skin on someone else's, releasing our juices onto and into them. Truly, each and every man, woman and child is an island unto

---

5. In a strange twist, we had a client completely consumed by the urge to meet Charles Dickens; Earle Upward was his name. We brought him back to the very beginning, to visit a young Charles, to play with blossoming genius. When it was time to return, he lost us. He escaped into the fabric of Victorian England. Reports from the edges of time, from scouts who explore the loose ends and hidden eddies, have gotten back to us over the years. Earle Upward shadowed Charles Dickens for a great part of his life, while disappearing more and more into the material of time. He tried everything to reach out and feel the author's dark overcoat, run his pale fingers through the man's hair and down along his body. There were moments of violence and moments where, completely unseen, he broke down and cried on the floor of the Dickens living room, tears of utter sadness fading before they ever hit the ground. Charles never made any indication of realizing Earle Upward's presence until one day, when sitting silently at his writing desk, he jerked, looking around and darting his eyebrows. When he was sure no one else was in the room, he stuck his tongue out and licked the air, while squinting. We have no way of knowing what he was thinking or whether Earle Upward had any presence of any kind left to him at that point, but that very night Charles Dickens pulled out a sheet of draft paper and began writing A Christmas Carol. I remind you, there is no such thing as non-fiction.

6. Any change in letter is, by definition, drastic. We have a mere 26, unlike some distant, obscure peoples and their ever-changing, uncountable characters. The average length of a word in the English language is 4.5 letters. That makes it impossible to have a perfectly average word. Except maybe "BELOU", where you can cut the "W" to a "U". The longest word is Imissthewayyouusedtosmilerightbeforewewenttobed, because it's more than a mile long. It seems that the longest word you can write with just the top row of the keyboard is rupturewort. But what kind of importance can the layout of the keyboard have on language? After enough years of typing miles of qwerty, will my children's children think in trapezoids? Will the letters array themselves, available to the two hands, so that 'saw' and 'was' become linguistically related as part of the same triangle and the vowels remain always ghettoized to the Northern row? Only A escapes the gulags... only A... Stop. Please excuse me. I've been accused before of prolixity. I find that sometimes the only thing I have left of her is words. Years of exchanges I can now only echo.

themselves, fixed and lonely in the archipelago of mankind."[7] In some ways this preacher is right, and to travel in time confirms it: we are a lonely species. But in some ways this is wrong. Pick up a great work of fiction and read the bedroom scene. Read it out loud, to a friend, to make it more concrete. Then pick up a tasteless piece of fiction and read the corresponding scene. The difference is in the language, not the acts. Maybe in one there is leather, maybe in another there are stains from fluids,[8] but there is a commonality of experience. The way her body moves under the fingers. The curve of the back and those sexual places where parts meet, anatomical seams. Someone (although I can always only ever picture her) gets up and uses the toilet with the door open, the partner watches from bed as they walk

---

7. The speech actually continues, although the content remains irrelevant to the manual. The Holy Roller continues, without pause: "But notice how my mouth moves when it makes the shapes of these words. There are physical consequences to the meaning of words. But these words, the 'tatterdemalions' and the 'concupiscents' and, say it with me, the 'voodoo.' Say it!" "Voodoo." Of the few people who have stopped to listen, only one or two mumble along. "I mean, really say them. Wrap your tongue around them! 'Auxiliary!'" The crowd grows, and with it, their enthusiasm. A deaf man watering his bright red flowers (begonias) two stories above looks down and sees a crowd stopped on the sidewalk, all stretching and flapping their mouths. He is reminded of the fable when greedy men turn to jackals and swine, braying and grunting, but also of the healing of the lepers. "Ergonomic!" "Ergonomic." "Grandiloquent!" "Grandiloquent." "Cuspidor!" "Cuspidor!" People are crying, and the black man is sweating and breathing between gasps. The sun smacks directly upon the divine heads. There is a howling and rending of garments, a gnashing of teeth, offerings of virgins and dramatic throes. The words have no meanings, but start to flow like a long loving raging river. "Vermillion!" "Vermillion!" "Potamophilous!" "Potamophilous!" The preacher throws up his hands, and the speaking in tongues and shouts of 'Hallelujah' die down. When he has silence, the preacher says, "Now I want you to mouth the words without making a sound. No air should pass through your pipes, no whispers. But if each of you makes the clicks and snaps of mouths moving, we will drown out the city itself, we will show these wounded streets with our flailing tongues that there is life as we wade through the ashes. Now, 'Hippopotomous.'" "Ee-pu-pu-na-mo." "Felicitous." "Eh-le-ee-ta." The deaf man joins the chorus, reading the smacking lips with cracked lenses, looking from above. "Anemone." "He-ne-pa-ne." "Umbrageous." "Um-pa-cha." Slowly a new language begins to form from what sounds like the crackle of a hundred silent smiles. Smile, right now, by yourself, wherever you are, and listen. Make these noises. People may watch, as they did the crowd. Embrace them, as the preacher does, in the new religion. And as the ecstasy hangs silkily in the air, he begins again, quietly: "They may say we are islands. They may say we are all passing through life alone. And is it hard? Nothing's harder. But we are not passing through, we are never passing by; there is no life that exists beyond us, beyond the harmony of our mouths. We do not pass through life, because life passes through our bodies! Look around you and see yourselves in unison. Nothing is ever permanently broken. You are alive, and you are one. This is the new benediction: Ee-pu-pu-na-mo eh-le-ee-ta he-ne-pa-ne um-pa-cha!" Two years later, on the same street corner, the preacher is shot by a disenfranchised follower. Witnesses say the last thing he shouts is, "Ephemera!" But it's too convenient. We went back. The last thing he said was, "Jejune."

8. And even then, there is no rule to which each of these belongs.

back naked. His mouth. Her eyes. Her hand. His thigh. The body parts, your body parts, her body parts[9] , are so interchangeable. The experience in time is like one of these parts. And because, in so many ways, our experiences are identical, Chrononavigation demands specificity. You want to revisit your honeymoon night? Easy, you think, because of how special it felt, because of uniqueness. A beach out the window, sand caught between his toes, a clumsily ripped condom wrapper on the nightstand and nerve endings sending frantic semaphores. You will suddenly find yourself in the bedroom of another couple, at another time. Your experience is the common experience. That's difficult to comprehend. You want to visit your dying father? How many different ways are there to die? Theoretically, an infinite. But there's a tendency towards conservativeness. Naturally? If you're American? Heart disease, cancer, melancholy, stroke, respiratory disease, cynicism, diabetes, pneumonia. These are our killers, the fellers of the anodyne. Even in suicides, of which there are statistically so few, most people are unimaginative. Self-mutilation, asphyxiation, those few of us brave enough to jump from a tall, tall place. If you cannot be specific, you will get caught in another lover's bedroom, near another old man's bathtub, under another teenager's dangling feet. There are so few ways to die, yet so many more ways to waste a life.

I will say this:
*BEWARE INTREPID CHRONONAUT*

Time travel is not for the faint of heart. There are certain things that arise; certain unexpected difficulties. I would like you to remember your father (my wife, her son, your anything). You finished making him his breakfast, had ground up the pills and spread them with the butter on the toast. It was the only way he'd actually take them. You call him a couple of times, but no response, not even a hint of noise. You went to check, making sure he's not simply tricking you.

---

9. The more stories I tell, the better the chance that I remember hers. Like cars in a junkyard they pile up, but I always hope to find a survivor, her surviving, trapped in the heap. I only ever dig up the desiccated reminders of someone else, which I swiftly discard. One day, she will step out of this oversaturated page.

You knocked on his bedroom door, no response. Not common but not uncommon. You open the door, first just a crack, without looking, to give him time to respond. Of course, he doesn't. You open the door and look in, and get an impression of a body slowly moving in the sweaty bedroom air. That's it. There are police, there are ambulances, there are graves and there is silence. You feel like a tragedy has occurred, but it's only accompanied by that impression; the movement of a body in a silent room. And in this there is serious danger. To illuminate, I wanted a pop-up illustration here, but it was rejected by my editor. [10]

Let me explain what my pop-up would have been: when you turned this last page, in front of you would have sprang a three dimensional room. It would have been assembled with photographic illustrations, a 3D photo of a bed, a 3D photo of a cat, perhaps... no, well, perhaps a dog... But hanging from the three dimensional rafter would be a life-like rope, and from that rope would hang a photograph of your father. His eyes would be bulging. His neck would be visibly broken, twisted too far. His tongue would be erect, peeling back lips to get out. One arm would hang quietly by his side, while the other would look unnaturally stiff, splayed out and turned in, somehow taxidermied-looking, or as if pinned down haphazardly, carelessly in an insect-display case. I would have used real rope, twine, really, so that as your hands shook beneath the covers of this manual, his body would flutter within the fixedness of the rest of the room. When you got so sick of looking at him you couldn't take it anymore, you'd turn the page, but the exact same pop-up would spring ever-so violently into your face. You'd start flipping through the book, trying to escape, and only after nine identical illustrations could you move on. Because what you might not realize now is that your brain was protecting you at the time. It didn't let you look back in that room. It didn't let you see that he was actually naked, those very last drops of urine teased from his penis forming splash patterns on the floor. Another way to think of it: when in a fit of uncomplicated clarity we touch a flame, we jerk

---

10. Too expensive to mass produce, he said. I have no respect for you, I said. He didn't seem to care. Time travel illustrates itself better than any representation, he said. He missed the point. This is the representation so that you're ready for the real thing.

our hand away, and after the initial hurt, only feel the burn when we're safely out of harm's reach. When you travel back, when you relive it, you don't get that grace period a second time. You can stand there and watch your father secure the rope. Watch him kick out the nightstand. Watch him writhe, and you better believe that writhing looks as bad as the word sounds. And you won't make anyone feel better when, in complete humiliation and terror, you vomit on your choking father.[11]  Of course, the fluid might disappear before it reaches him, but the damage is done. You cannot look away, you cannot stop him, and you cannot save him. This is why we recommend taking anti-nausea medication before your trip.

Before progressing:
*A BRIEF, NON-TANGENTIAL FORAY INTO THE HISTORY OF OUR ORGANIZATION*

Exactly two thousand years after the birth of Jesus Christ, a homeless man known only as Hunky Dory Rory was found lying in the streets of New York City, half frozen and more than half drunk, almost all dead. The police took extra pity on him, given the holiday spirit, and drove him to the hospital. The technicians in the emergency room revived him, but the doctor on call, a curiously named P.V. Lazurus, had a feeling in his gut that the man was suffering beyond the smack of intoxication and humility. After a number of blood tests, Rory was diagnosed with a rare degenerative disease. One technician joked, "I could have told you he was a degenerate before the tests." Everyone laughed except Lazurus, who returned to the emergency room to give his patient the Christmas tidings. Hunky Dory Rory sighed, rubbed his hands back and forth over his greasy scalp, and asked if he could

---

11. In reality, only around a third of the people who have medical side effects are affected in this way. A good number more have reported a strange sensation, in which they become suddenly aware of their own anatomies. They can feel their lungs pumping oxygen into the blood, their blood circulating, their heart beating, their kidney's producing urine, the liver secreting bile, the glands of the skin producing oil and sweat… The mechanisms that keep us going all suddenly seem so fragile. Indeed, to say the "mechanisms that keep us going" denies the real crisis: that these base biological processes are us. And we are fragile. That's difficult to handle, especially as your father is softly gasping for his last breath. We are so, so fragile.

use the telephone. Dr. Lazurus nodded and led the dying man into his office, saying he could use it as long as he liked. Rory thanked him, and then realized that it was the first time he'd thanked anyone in years. Sitting at the desk, he picked up the telephone, and, with one slow, confused digit, punched the numbers into the console. The phone rang. A record of the conversation was recalled much later and transcribed[12] , but the outcome was that our founder, Professor Saul Wyle discovered that not only was his father still alive, but that he was possibly carrying his own genetic downfall. When he decided to go through with the tests, he found, in what was the second worst day of his life that he most likely had less than a decade to live. After walking around Central Park for fourteen hours, he went back to his apartment, and sat down, and started thinking. He wrote down notes and scribbles on his many note pads, then in the margins of books, finally resorting to the backs of receipts and tax returns. From his window, he decoded the changing of the seasons, the patterns of the traffic (foot and motor), the intricate repetition in the flights of the pigeons (an entire volume is filled with arrows and the constantly repeated words: flap flap flap shit flap flap flap flap eat eat eat flap flap eat flap flap shit shit), the sacred design that revealed itself in the stones of the sidewalk

---

12. "Hello?"
"Is this Saul?"
"Who is this?"
"Is this Saul?"
"I told you already, I'm not interested—"
"This is your father."
 6.1 seconds of silence.
"I'm dying."
Strangely, exactly 6.1 more seconds of silence.
"You died already."
"Circumstantially. Now absolutely."
Too many emotions coursed through him in too few seconds. "You've no right... Where are you? I don't... I've got money, I've got friends who are doctors..."
"I'm not calling because I want help. I'm calling because I wanted to tell you that I might be killing you too. Get some blood tests. Be sure."
"What?"
"I'm a toxic asset."
"What?"
"I'm sorry. I need to go."
"No... please... please, please, please, jesus dad, please, please, jesus, don't go."
The conversation ends.

when stared at for hours on end, the order of the sounds of the city, the cycle of the license plates that passed by... In the end, the Professor had perfectly charted and planned the pattern of the city, a codex of its movements and mutterings, its complex heaving, and it was only a small step to extend his algorithm to the flow of time. Already a man of some renown and means, he established a small company completely devoted to making real the possibility of time travel, even as his body betrayed itself. Professor Wyle and his team, of which I was an original member, were mavericks, for while it's something we feel comfortable with now, at the beginning, Chrononavigation was uncharted territory. We were frontiersmen. And it was in a small office with that handful of friends that time was conquered. Or tamed. Or understood. The first successful travel through time occurred on the first day of the eleventh month, ten years after Saul Wyle received that fateful call.[13] It was only a little while later, after some of the darker questions and considerations were dealt with and the proper authori-

---

13. This first exploration was nine years into the past, where Saul Wyle visited his father, Hunky Dory Rory, in his final moments. Back on the streets and looking for a quiet and inoffensive place to die, Rory woke up one morning in downtown Manhattan to a roar that seemed to come from below him. He emerged bleary-eyed from the doorway of the discothèque where he'd been sleeping to see a billow of thick black smoke streaming from a building down the street from him. He squinted, his face filling with sudden dread, and began to unevenly lope away from the explosion. A block later, he stopped, and started swirling his head around, to crack his neck and upper back. "Fuck it," his son later heard him say time after time, and Hunky Dory Rory turned around and ran back towards the billows of smoke. It was difficult, when he got closer, to push against the tides of running people, but he managed to make it right to the base of the towers before they fell directly on top of him. The last thing he said, choking on smoke and staring straight up, was, "I thought everyone else was going to die before me." His son cried the first dozen times he watched the fall, but then started feeling peaceful during it. The last time he jumped back to watch it, he actually smiled, and stroked the air near his father's head. Coming back into the present, he arranged for his own death. Saul Wyle, the first Chrononaut, knew most of the limitations and laws that govern the art, but wanted, as a last act, to try to defy them. He gave explicit instructions to the programmers. In the day before his death, they were to launch him back to the very beginning, the Big Bang, the separation of the prime colors, the creation of all things. He wanted to watch the entirety of history, not able to play god, but to at least maybe shadow his hand. We knew that he would slowly disintegrate into the stream of time, at some point giving his consciousness up completely to the flow, but he thought that it might be possible that millions of years later, when Rory Wyle watched his wife give birth to their first and only child, the dispersed elements might suddenly come crashing back together into his just-born being, and that he would live forever in a long, undecipherable loop. Because it was his final wish, nobody dared utter the word "futility" around him, more than happy to provide their modern-day prophet with his last request. On the day proposed for the launch, however, the Professor failed to show up. It was only the next day that his body was discovered on the aforementioned merry-go-round. I saw it, and for the first time in my life, I understood the vastness of infinity and the smallness of that other thing which we have.

ties mollified, that services opened to the public.

*SOME FURTHER LIMITATIONS AND REFLECTIONS:*

Time travel is lonely. Deeply and darkly lonely in ways that, I promise, you have never felt before in your worst hour. We can prepare you for anything; that's my job, to make you as prepared as you can possibly be, that's what we're doing right now, but so far no one has figured out a way to jump together. You will reach out, I promise, to try to grab the hand of someone, feel something human in the strange, inhuman past. You will touch nothing, because there's nothing to touch. "Time travel is loneliness," Professor Wyle once said. "It's just you standing before the unending..." [14] We cannot prepare you for this.

Another warning. Do not time travel to prove anything.

One more warning, if you will continue to listen. You must understand that standing before time, there cannot exist the comforting

---

14. Days before he died, he provided the best, if least lucid description of what the sensation is like. "Imagine, if you will," he said, "A theater. Or more like a stadium. Somewhere, there is this giant stadium. Vast and tall, it can fit hundreds of thousands of souls. Then imagine the stadium that surrounds that stadium. It holds millions. Rings of concentric stadiums tower out until the select few in the smallest look up and see only blurred faces, not stars. Then, in the very center of all of this is a tiny stage, empty except for a single object. This is a large tank of water. It is a perfectly clear rectangle of glass, the dimensions of a small but tall room. Inside this tank, there is a perfectly clear plastic sack. Crouched fetus-like inside is a man holding a microphone. He remains dry, despite the water around him. A small, clear cord runs from the mouth of the bag to the surface of the water, providing a source of air for the man. At an unspoken sign, the thunderous chorus of quietly murmuring spectators and crinkling of concessions bags dies down. The man begins to recite these words, slowly and precisely, and he repeats them again and again while they ricochet around the layers of stadiums: 'I am the mailman of Venice. Give me a coin, and I will show you these streets. I am the mailman of Venice, and only I know the ways and waters of this city. Give me a coin and I'll show you the tongue of Saint Anthony, the heart of Saint Agony, and the clit of Saint Somebody.' Nearly three hours pass before the man stops his recitation. It takes another hour and a half for the last echoes to fade from the countless stadiums. After minutes of silence, the man curls up even further in his bag, and the crowd quietly empties the stadium, father's hugging their sons closer to them, mother's kissing their daughters' foreheads. In the darkness, the only sounds in the stadium are the man's amplified, underwater respirations. A breeze carries a candy wrapper from under a vacant seat onto the surface of the water, where it drifts lazily across to a corner. And this is the loneliness of time travel." His detractors called him the Enigmatic Prick for a reason. Indeed, in those final days he called himself the Memphis Crustacean, and nobody could figure out why. But then again, nobody asked. And nobody ever took the time to understand what he was saying.

rites and passages of a priest.[15]   Time strips from us the classic mitigating narrators. You cannot understand its rawness.

You are now ready to move onto basic training.  Before you go, I'd like you to imagine one last thing.  A beautiful woman in a room flooded with warm sunlight.  Don't leave her a concept.  Fill in the details.  Make her your own; make the room your own.  She has filled the room with tulips, swirling pale orange accented with pink.  Or some other color, if you like.  She is so slight, like something possibly not there, and has dark brown hair.  Or not.  She sits in a chair with a very straight back, informing her posture.  She sits in that chair for days and days.  The tulips quickly extend to full blossom, and then continue unchecked, distending and warping as their water dries up.  Seeing the past… There is an eloquence of objects in these stories, you understand?  Sitting with her again, you can't leave her, and everything slowly loses its meaning.  Like when you stare at a word for too long, and it loses all value, receding back into the depths of meaningless markings.  Only once dead petals begin to fall does she react, moving as if in gelatin or formaldehyde.  Every time you see her, all you want is to touch her, to undo your mistakes.  And all I ever grab is air. continue unchecked, distending and warping as their water dries up.  Seeing the past… There is an eloquence of objects in these stories, you understand?  Sitting with her again, you can't leave her, and everything slowly loses its meaning.  Like when you stare at a word for too long, and it loses all value, receding back into the depths of meaningless markings.[16]  Only once dead petals begin to fall does she react, moving as if in gelatin or formaldehyde.  Every time you see her, all you want is to touch her, to undo your mistakes.  And all I ever grab is air.

---

15. Don't visit Jesus. There is too much randomness. The pilgrims, who when the technology became public, poured through our gates, suddenly found that they'd traveled millennia to see a human subjected to inhuman violence. One man described it as "pornographic voyeurism." Another came back and stared blankly at me and said, "I don't get it." Another only chuckled while she settled her bill, a curiously self-satisfied noise. You can believe whatever you will, but you can only see what there is.

16. My dreams have changed, in recent years. They are intensely vivid, but less in my control. The sex and the loneliness are more violent than ever before, but for the first time in my life, I've been waking up bitter, upset that it's not my reality. Because even as you discover that nothing fits nicely in its boundaries, that everything spills into the margins, that you cannot help getting your hands dirty, that meanings lustily jumble behind your back and outside your gaze, you know that nothing goes on forever.

# The Windowsillhouette

*Alashiya Gordes*

Nine time. The alarm clock ticks from far, the slowest bone-beat of the ear. The tick speaks, and all the world is shallow. All except the hollow. To this, the tick creeps. It rains, but remains dry – a window breaks the weather. Whether that will be a Thing or no is for Snow White herself to know.

Now one had probably properly describe her as Off White, but she'd likely dislike that. If it was a girl, she was surely lying. A right down lie, with the flattest stomach of the world, and smooth as a hairbrushed magazine. Anyway, she was lying. Ivory and lying. No wind rose, no breath rose, no thorn had risen, either. Just the rain and headless, you know, no long, soft hair to gleam and blow, she had nowhere else to go but lie between those walls. Head, leg, arm – none. Never there, never gone. Nor breasts; just belly. An alabaster belly.

Her argument hinges on the pit of her stomach, you see. It will not lift (and her having no arms, this doesn't much surprise). The hands of the alarm must do to prick, but, as short, send out the tick to work the dirty for them. It will not lift, and at the front, even falls right in. It's quite the oddest navel in the world, and that's a thing hard come by. The bottom of this tip is grubbier than one thinks, and the tick thinks it has tall walls as it whips its itching ear like a dog with a hind leg. Having two more pairs than she should do, it makes up for the lipless girl. Some lips, tick – atta baby, here we go…

It sits. It waits. It eats, it weights. Her mother pricks a finger? Droplet doesn't linger long. It falls down, soft feather down, to the wood-dust nest.

That was for the best, for all the rest would make a nasty contrast. There it wasn't seen. That place would never clean. Anyway. So once upon a chime, Snow White's silly mother sewed. Some stories saw it snow. This one says it rained. The drops' fists punched the pane. Tick, hold out your tongue again! Her sillhouette is wet again. Tock; they live without all pain, if never after 9am.

# Caravan
## *Elizabeth MacNeal*

For almost as long as Lily could remember, or as long as she wanted to remember, the twisted remains of the old cream caravan had sat at the bottom of her garden. Her sister Maisie treated it like a climbing frame, crawling over the foaming sofa padding and stirring grass in a dented pan over the hob. The linoleum was falling apart even more than it had been before, coursed through with a crawling network of weeds. Lily and Jason were older and understood, and tried to get their mother to stop her. It was a hazard, an accident waiting to happen, and before long the rotten floor would give way and the caravan would collapse on pink, feathery tutu-clad Maisie.

Lily was six when her father had bought the caravan at a second-hand auction, the kind of auction which he never took Lily along to, as it was only suitable for Jason, who was nine and a boy. Sometimes, pushed by the incessant probing of his sister, he would reveal tantalising details of the smell of oil, hot dogs and swearing men who drank pint after pint of warm beer, and Lily would shiver with delight. Her father went every week and came back stinking of sweat and booze and grease, trailing his wide-eyed son, but this time she knew that something special had happened.

Jason was back later than usual, and they could hear the dull grumble of her father's anger, pierced by her mother's shouting. Maisie was asleep in her cot, breathing hoarsely and snuffling occasionally.

"You smell funny," Lily whispered. She was hot and clammy with anticipation, and had been sitting on the bottom bunk reading with her torch.

"It's beer," Jason said, proudly. "Dad let me have a pint."

Lily inhaled sharply. "What was it like?" She breathed in the sweet, clammy smell of beer on his breath. "Are you drunk?"

"Of course not. You can't get drunk on only one beer, stupid."

"What was it like?"

"Oh, I dunno, I liked it. I'd had it before, though."

Lily leaned forward. "What else happened?"

He paused emphatically, and then said, "I'm not allowed to tell. It's a secret." In the dark, he puffed out his chest.

"Please? I won't tell anyone."

"It doesn't matter. Anyway, you might. I know what you're like."

Lily was offended. "What d'you mean? I've never told anyone any of your secrets! Not even the one about..."

"Shhhh!" he hissed, even though he knew that there was no one listening. "That's what I mean! Anyway, women can't be trusted."

His sister snorted. "Says who?"

"Dad did. Women can't keep secrets, he said, and he's always right."

Lily was unsure what to say. Faced with such authority, she wondered if it might have been true. If it was a simple and factual matter of her gender, then there was very little she could do to prove herself worthy. She decided to try again. "I promise I won't tell. Remember I told you about the time that with Mum, you know," she lowered her voice. "Was... kissing," she looked about furtively. "Was kissing the garage man."

Jason had to admit it was true, and there was a silence as he tried to refute it. He pulled the frayed knot of his pyjamas, winding it round his pinkie until his fingertip bulged white. "But you told me about it didn't you? You didn't keep it a secret, did you? You told. What if you told someone else my secret? Then it wouldn't be a surprise." He sighed, drawing the covers up to his chin and nudging her with her foot. "Anyway, go to sleep. I'm tired."

"Please?" she asked again, nudging him back.

"No," he said, suddenly cold. "Stop asking questions. I'll push you off the bunk." From past experience, Lily knew that he would be true to his word. Admittedly, it had been the cat that had last been flung from the top bunk in a furry tumble, but only because Lily herself had refused to move, and Jason knew that it was weak to fail to carry out threats.

She slept fitfully that night, wondering what dark and interesting thing Jason could possibly be concealing. At breakfast, she tried to ignore Jason's hastily obscured conspiratory winks and knowing chuckles, which his father ignored. He was smoking a cigarette, paper sprawled in front of him. He stubbed it out on a tablecloth, which was plastic and pock-marked with singed burn marks.

"John, please," her mother said.

He shrugged. "It's broken anyway. I bought it." She sighed loudly, clanking the blackened pot and stirring the porridge.

"How long's the bloody breakfast going to be, anyway?"

She sighed again, inhaling as though to reply, and then thinking better of it. Jason had shaken salt on to the table and was pushing it into a mound.

"Don't do that," his mother said.

"Why the bloody hell shouldn't he?" John answered, and angrily shook some on to the tablecloth. Jason grinned. The shaker was smooth china covered in snaking roses, which were faded and had rubbed off in places. It had been a present which Lily had bought her mother for her birthday, and she had stolen a pound coin from the back pocket of her father's jeans. When he had broken the matching pepper pot, Lily had cried. She didn't cry often because he smacked her for it.

"Here we go, Dad," she said, putting the chipped china bowl in front of him. Jason had his own one, which was plastic and had "Jason" written in waving and uncertain lines. In the middle was a crudely-drawn skull and crossbones. The porridge was glutinous and covered with a yellow layer of melted butter.

He grunted his thanks. "Anything good in the paper?" he asked his father, even though he wasn't interested.

His father shrugged. "Nah. Lost to Birmingham last week, though."

"Oh?" said Lily, and Jason shot her a look of disdain.

"What would you know about it anyway? You're a girl."

"That doesn't mean I don't know anything. I'm better at maths than you, and I'm a whole two years younger." Lily was cleverer than her brother and knew it.

"Yeah right. You don't know anything." He spat the words. "Anything."

"Will you two shut the bloody hell up?" her father said, and Jason looked embarrassed. He narrowed his eyes at Lily.

Her mother pulled the chair away from the table and sat down. "What are you doing to do with the kids today?"

"Seeing David," John muttered.

She looked exasperated. "You said you'd watch the kids! I've got to work. I told you about this weeks ago!" She shook her head.

"For God's sake, it's fine. It's not like we need to be looked after. We're not babies," Jason said, although he looked crestfallen. The blasphemy seemed to clunk in his voice, and he longed for the authority his father had when he said it.

"You heard the boy," John answered, shoving the porridge into the side of his mouth as he spoke. "I won't be long. Just got things to do." Jason smiled at him. "Will you stop grinning like one of those fucking special kids?" he said, and his mother narrowed her eyes at him. "What the hell are you gawping at?" She averted her gaze quickly.

They sat in silence for the rest of the meal, the only sound the clink of spoon on china, and the thud, thud, thud of Jason's foot against the chair leg.

"I'll be back before four," her mother said. "Unless it's a quiet day and Mark lets me go early. Anyway, you've got my mobile number." Jason looked puzzled. "Yes you do, it's on the noticeboard, and if it's important, you can look up the number of the supermarket in the phonebook. Wait, I'll write it on the back of this envelope for you." It was only when she was on the bus that she remembered that the phone had been disconnected the week before.

Lily didn't mind being left alone, and could spend hours lost in her thoughts. Their garden wasn't large, was just a rectangular patch walled in by a thatched fence on one side and a beech hedge on the other – put up by the neighbours – but was so overgrown that it seemed like a jungle. It reminded Lily of the sort of gardens she had read about in books, where there were rusty old keys hidden under bushes, and tin boxes containing hidden relics that someone had buried before the war. There was an apple tree in the corner, but it only produced knobbly apples, brown and soft with wasps, which made Lily pull a face they were so sour. In the corner was an old pram, turned upside down and surrounded by soft stinging nettles.

Lily had a doll, a rag doll called Rosemary Primose with one button eye and one stitched eye, and fluffy wool hair from where she had unwound it, and she sat with her at the bottom of the garden. There was a vague stone path which wormed its way down to old wooden gates which backed on to the road. They pretended to drink tea, or rather muddy water, from cracked terracotta pots. Their table was an overturned crate, and Lily had trampled the nettles and weeds to create a little hollow for their secret meetings. Rosemary Primrose liked to swing on the wire of the discarded washing line, and trek through the jungle in order to find her real parents. She was adopted, as Lily would explain to anyone who would listen.

She was interrupted by Jason's jeering. He had grown bored of sitting in front of the fuzzy old television and was feeling irritable and wanted to tease her. Maisie was sleeping upstairs and he couldn't be bothered to wake her.

"Dare you to touch a stinging nettle," he said, and picked a handful.

"No," Lily said, turning her back on him and shielding Rosemary Primrose from him. She had a fluffy wound on her arm from where he had operated on her in a spiteful game of doctors and nurses.

"I will," he said, and picked it up in the middle where he knew it wouldn't sting. It was a trick he had learnt from his best friend Oliver.

Lily scrutinised his face for a flinch and he dropped it. "See? Doesn't hurt," he said, and showed her his fingertips where there were no white or red pimples.

"Well, I don't want to," she said, decisively.

"You're boring," he replied, and grabbed Rosemary Primrose from her hand, throwing her into the corner of the garden, separated from Lily by a thick bank of stinging nettles. She landed with a soft thump and then a crash as they gave way.

"I bet you're going to cry now," Jason said, and laughed.

She didn't say anything, but stared at him with a look of hatred. He shrugged and turned away, sauntering back down the path and into the house.

When the caravan arrived, it was raining and Lily was sobbing, thigh-deep in stinging nettles. Her arms were bobbly with the hot white stings of the nettles as she pushed through them, trying to find her ragdoll. The noise in the street outside surprised her, as it was a dead-end alleyway and none of their neighbours had cars. Her family did, but her father rarely used it as it wasn't taxed, and was old and faded pink and made a roaring noise when he accelerated.

Jason ran down the drive, pulling aside the rotten gates and shouting with glee. "Look Lily!" he said, and she forgot the pain of the stinging nettles for a moment. "Look what Dad's got us!"

The caravan was faded white, stained black in places, with a heavy beige line which ran round the middle, broken by the windows which had torn lace curtains. Her father honked the horn, and his enthusiasm was contagious.

"What d'you think?" he asked as she circled it in delight.

"Oh, it's brilliant." She paused, running her finger along a quivering crack which ran from the right wheel to the bottom of the cream windowsill, the sort of crack that made Lily think of the sound of screeching chalk on a blackboard whenever she looked at it. "But it's broken," she said. Her father scratched his head and sighed.

"It still works alright. I'll fix her up as good as new."

"Can we look inside?" Lily asked, pulling at the door.

He pulled a key out of his pocket, a little silver key that looked like it was far less important than it was. The interior was faded and old, a torn sofa gushing foam in the corner, and two bunks with urine-stained mattresses. To Lily, it was perfect.

"Can we go on holiday?" she asked, excitedly.

Jason was standing still, next to his father. "Of course, idiot. Why else would we have bought it? So it can sit in the garden?"

"That's enough," her father said, and she smiled proudly at the fact that, for once, he had stood up for her. Jason kicked a stone angrily with the scuffed end of his trainers

"Can I bring Mr Nibbles? He'll be good."

"Yes, bring bloody Mr Nibbles. As long as he doesn't eat through any of the sofa." Lily didn't like to point out that it looked like it was half-eaten already. "D'you think Mum'll like it?"

"She'll love it," Lily said, with certainty, and her father smiled. All afternoon, he felt as excited and childlike as Lily and Jason, jumping whenever he heard the door. Lily's mother was late back from work, tired and red-nosed from the cold. Lily and Jason danced around her feet, tugging her arms as they led her down the wobbling stepping stones, over the weeds and past the nettles where Rosemary Primrose lay forgotten.

But when they removed the blindfold, she cried and clenched her tummy under white fingers. "What the hell have you done now?" she said, not angrily but bitterly, stroking the rounded lump under her apron. "We can barely afford the fucking rent!" Her father recoiled as though he'd been punched.

"I thought you'd like it! Look, take a look inside. You'll like it inside. There are two beds, and the sofa makes a third. It's perfect. We can go up north, we can take a break and go on holiday, look!" he tugged her roughly by the wrist.

"Let go of me!" she said, and shook her wrist free. The imprint of his hand left a thick red rim on her arm. "Don't you fucking touch me! How the hell can we afford it? I work overtime as it is. And what with this thing," she motioned at her tummy, "Oh god, how the fuck are we going to live?" She was crying, her face red and blotchy, and her tears mingled with the rain.

Her father slammed his fist heavily against the door, and the metal shuddered, puckered inwards. "I was only doing it to be fucking nice! Some fucking thanks I get." He turned to Jason, who was staring at him with scared, wide eyes. "What the fuck are you looking at?" he spat, and swung clumsily at him. He fell instantly, blood dribbling out of his nose on to the gravel.

Lily and her mother walked back into the house leaving him standing there, back arched against the door, sobbing. It wasn't the sobbing of a child, or a woman, but the pained, forced sobbing of a man, in gasps which seemed to wrench his body in two.

They left Jason, sprawled on the ground with his bloody school-boy knees and wistful expression.

"Dad, are you alright?" Jason asked tentatively, still looking at the ground. His father ignored him, and kicked the door, harder this time. The cream rim bent under it, and he drove his hand through the glass of the window, clenching his fist which was paint red and bristled with broken glass. His anger suddenly abated, and quite calmly, he unlocked the door of his rusty old road-taxless car, and started the engine. Jason stood up unsteadily

"Dad, wait. I'll come with you. Take me with you," Jason said, panic in his voice, and ran to the door. His father leaned over to the passenger door, and pushed the lock down. And he hit the accelerator, and through the rear-view window watched, between the swinging fluffy dice, his son with his bloody nose and knees, legs pounding like pistons as he chased him down the street.

# Monse Flying Away

## Fibian Lukalo

We all crowded hidden behind the school library attentively listening to Duile with our eyes all fixed on the object he was holding. No-one else could share the seriousness and urgency of this meeting since we had suffered as a class for too long. "Wait for me, woi ye... woi ye," loudly cried plump Vengi as she cruised towards the group with all the speed her body could go, even though she was the slowest runner in our class. Everyone was here, even short Monse, who had just come back after three weeks from his father's funeral. Oh, he looked very, very, very sad as his bald shaven head shone in the hot morning sun! Will "matatus" (public transport cars) continue to kill our parents?

One Monday morning Monse's father was travelling back from their rural home to work here in Eldoret when the matatu he was using rammed into a stationary petrol tanker. "He is suffering, he is suffering," was all Monse used to whisper constantly as his eyes stared blankly. And, when BBC Samson told us he had overheard from his mother that Monse's father's head was badly burnt and that he was sure to die we all told him to keep quite. "Oh shut up, you loud mouth," shouted Cara, the tallest girl in our class, and BBC Samson ran out of the class, since we had all learnt that when Cara shouts it was best to duck! Sometimes, we found BBC Samson's mouth was too long and his ears were even longer like that time, did he not know it was sad to lose a father? Did he not know it was wrong to talk about someone dying or death? My grandmother told me once that death could hear and answer and so we were never to talk about it.

Did BBC Samson not hear Monse say his father was in the hospital ICU, a place nearest to God? Then BBC Samson said that ICU was the place we all went to as we waited for space in heaven or coming back to earth. He was horrible! But two days later BBC Samson was proved right and I saw him walk around the class with the – I told you – swagger which was exaggerated by his squeaky torn shoes.

Coming from his three weeks of absence we were happy to see Monse return. Before then we all thought that he would not come back just like Bosy and Elly, who had lost their mothers. So that morning we spent most of our morning prep lesson listening to Monse's terrifying funeral stories and even then I still did not get to hear or know how the ICU was nearest God. Monse seemed confused but I could tell he missed his father. He told us of the midnight scary journey to their rural home with the corpse covered in a black "jwala" (polythene paper) atop a Peugeot Saloon. He kept on thinking that his father must have felt cold in the huge coffin, and he said it made him cry. But, his aunt kept on telling him, "You are the first born, why are you crying? Dry your tears, do you want to follow your father?" From then on Monse said he was very scared and did not move near his father's coffin.

Monse also told us of his many relatives, old, young, wearing all manners of clothes and who spent most of the time crying, dancing to "isukuti" (drums) and "litungu" (lyre), endless cooking and even scolding his mother! "Huge pots of food and African beer was there, and you know the way my father never took beer," said Monse. On the burial day Monse and his siblings were hidden and so he never got to see his father buried: "By then I was so scared and tired, I could have hidden myself only if they had asked." When Duile asked for the reason, Monse told us it was bad, very bad. But Duile thought that it was bad because of the bad dreams about dead people. Only Cara seemed to have a reason and she said that one child in her village had jumped into the open grave so that was why children were kept away. We had to accept this, since it was not the time to reason with Cara. All the while Monse kept on rubbing his eyes and crying until they were very red.

Quickly, before we knew it, Duile took up his "pastor" duty and jumped up shouting and praying fervently for Monse. He asked Monse to kneel and we all formed a circle around them with Duile casting out all evil dreams and things disturbing him. Duile continued to jump up, banging his hand on the desk and shouting continuously, "Shetani ashindwe! Shetani ashindwe!" ("The devil is defeated"); he became even louder and turned darker as we all chorused back loudly, "Ameni, ameni" ("Amen"). Then Vengi rushed into the class breathless carrying her huge Mickey Mouse patched bag, which was always filled with broken cookies from the local bakery, to warn us that Mrs Ona was heading our direction. Faster than the fearful Turkana watchmen's arrows we were all seated and reading our pastoral education books.

Mrs Ona, our class teacher, walked into class in a quiet way with a crooked smile – by then we were buried in our books reading seriously. Suddenly she announced, "I want the list of noisemakers from Vengi." Instantly, we all turned back to look at Vengi, then at Mrs Ona and then, frightened, all at each other. Then we all started complaining at the same time in different languages, upon which Mrs Ona's nose flared: "Keep quiet and what things are you saying, you will all remain behind today after school for extra work." Vengi's voice could be heard protesting above all our murmurs; soon she ran off to the toilet, and as usual she could stay there even for one lesson. Our complaints were cut short by the clang of our old school bell, which BBC Samson once told me was as old as his dead uncle who had learnt in our school in 1934! Just how old was our school? BBC Samson even said that his uncle's name was inscribed in one of the boys' toilets as "Tough Man-mguu" (leg). I continued to look at my pastoral book, and glanced over to where Monse sat and saw him lying head down on his desk. Could he still be sleepy and tired from all that he had seen and done? Mrs Ona waddled slowly up to him and whispered something to him and then loudly asked us all to pray for him. "Pray for Monse, he needs to come back to school," she told us. If only she would have asked us, we had already done that but no-one dared since we now had a punishment to think about.

Vengi turned up looking sick halfway through the next lesson, maths. While the rest of the class giggled as she explained to the teacher that her stomach was aching, I heard my desk-mate giggle, "…girls eat too much so they stay long outside…it's adolescence… we know those things…" But today I ignored him since my arrival time at home had been changed, and I kept thinking and wondering about Monse and how it felt to lose a father and have a punishment. As the maths teacher interestingly showed us new formulas for areas of triangles, everyone seemed alert and participated happily in the work. Therefore, when he proceeded to give us two pages of homework, no one complained. We knew it would also take him two weeks to ask for the books and another two to mark them. It was during such interesting lessons, and especially before the PE class, that we were rarely attentive.

BBC Samson would be extremely quiet, pretending to pay attention but really counting the minutes ticking away. Footballer Ero kept tapping on his desk with one leg, the other sticking out of his seat ready to run out of class. Mrs Ona constantly punished him for his poor work but he kept on saying "I will be a famous footballer one day, just like Didier Drogba, and by then Mrs Ona would be long dead." During such a maths lesson, the "supus" (belles) of the class, led by Jossie, kept passing pieces of notes to and fro, each note decreasing or increasing their group members. I never liked them at all, since I needed to buy the lipstick sold by the thuggish-looking hawker and Johnson's baby powder in order to join the group. My mother, oh that mama would not allow that! Jossie believed she was the most beautiful girl in class and that all boys were hers. She only picked the big tall boys not short ones like Monse, BBC Samson and those who smelt of urine! Duile scared her so much because he had prophesied her long hair would be damaged by hair chemicals. I hated it most when Jossie would force some girls to bring her money, especially carefree Halima who always did just that. Even after one year of receiving lots of money they had not accepted Halima into their group. Times like this I was happy we had tomboy Cara in our class, otherwise Jossie and her group would have eaten our heads!

Come the physical education lesson we scrambled to leave the class and got stuck in the doorway as we struggled to leave. Duile announced, "Let's meet behind the library after the PE lesson, I have something very important for all of us." Off Ero, the class prefect, zoomed to get the football and Jossie the skipping ropes for the girls. She always did this to control the game! I could hear hearty laughter coming from the teachers seated in the staff room, since the tea break session would be soon, and I quickly ducked and ran towards the playing field to avoid any teacher's watchful eye. Getting the attention of the teacher was a disaster, since one would spend most of the lesson buying buns for them, and other niceties they wanted from the canteen at the far end of the school.

Unfortunately, for the girls there were no skipping ropes and so Mrs Ona told us to all play football. Dividing the class into two teams wasn't easy: all the boys argued at the same time, rules were set and re-set, and above all Ero jumped up and down blowing his whistle noisily and exposing his cowboy brand underwear until Vengi developed a headache. Finally, after several wasted minutes, Ero realised that he would miss his football game and said there would be two teams, boys versus girls, and the girls would be allowed two goalkeepers. "Hurray! Hurray!" shouted bow legged Ambla, and Jossie asked him to "shh" because he was a nuisance with his noise and urine-soaked shorts. By then, I could see that Vengi and Monse were not feeling too fine so they were selected to be the goalkeepers. Girls had a tough time fitting Vengi with the football boots and pads but finally she squeezed into them promising to keep alert. I was the assistant goalkeeper, together we tried out some pre-match warm-up exercises as the boys jeered. I really wondered if we would save any shots as Ero yelled and terrified us from the centre of the field, "Wait for our hot shots, your hands will tear apart today! Monse loved football; as he took up his post confidently, we all clapped and cheered him on. The boys exaggerated and roared him on with shouts of "man power, man power." Then he seemed ten feet tall and I watched and wondered whether, at eleven years of age, he would stay with us long enough to play more football matches .For now all we had to share was this noisy football match.

Our football match didn't need a referee, we all knew the rules, so when Duile shouted "GO," the boys' team fired right away. Much as they tried, no shot was scored by the boys that day. Vengi's headache lessened as the match became exciting and she even tried to side-step one boy only to tumble with a thud with her uniform tearing at the side-seam. If I had not been quick with my legs, oh! it would have been a score, but alas I ran, stretched and kicked the ball with all my might halfway down the field and all the girls' cheered wildly, "Yeah! Yeah! Girl power girl power, we are tough." Almost immediately, Ambla stopped the ball and he pulled back and gave it a big kick that saw the ball zoom way above our goalpost and land into the forbidden flowerbeds. His team-mates shouted at him "Usitumie ugali…wacha ugali…tumia mchele…mchele" ("Don't use all your force, be soft be soft"). From that moment on every time Ambla touched the ball the field would be rent with cries of "mchele…mchele," pleading with him to be softer on the ball.

Our team needed a score urgently since time was running out, so every time I got the ball I kicked it as hard as I could, aiming at the centre of the field. This time I was lucky since Hamida was running in the direction of the goal and her long Borana legs carried her so fast that Monse did not see her coming. As Ero and the other fast boys tried to cut into her path, she gave the ball one strong kick, which hit Duile on his shoulder and as he twisted around to turn direction, the ball flew past Monse into the goal. "Goal! Goal! Goal! Halima juu! Halima juu!" all the girls screamed and ran towards her. We took as much time rejoicing over the goal, as the boys congregated and discussed new tactics. However, we would have to continue the match another time since the old bell clanged and Duile shouted aloud, "Meeting, meeting, lib…lib…" Anyone watching us keenly would have seen a hurried beeline towards the library.

This boy Duile really surprised me! Many times he would own up to doing some form of mischief, even when he wasn't involved and he would be punished for the whole class's mistake. Duile did not like seeing teachers punish us for mistakes we did or did not do. So just like today, when Mrs Ona wanted to punish the noise makers he stood up and said, "It's me Madam;" even when Mrs Ona questioned how he could have made such noise he still repeated, "It was me Madam," and I found that very strange. Strange because Duile had many times washed the classroom, cut the long grass, remained behind after school and even washed the boys' smelly toilets, yet most of the time he was innocent! Today I wondered what big plans he had for us. I did not know what to expect and imagined he would go into his "pastor" healing for the class as he had done for Halima when she ate the raw guavas. On that day he asked Halima, as if threatening her, if she believed in the man of God. Then he asked Halima to kneel in the centre of the class, and as she knelt in the class receiving healing prayers, Mrs Ona watched him from the door and for once he was caught in a mistake and fairly punished.

No, even then he pleaded with the teacher to let Halima go home early since he was the man of God and she had been very sick. The next day Halima brought Duile a kilogram of sugar in appreciation for her cure, he accepted it but gave it out to the school's Turkana watchman. Duile was the tallest and darkest boy in our standard six class; his father, a notable councillor, was also quite rich and they owned a shop nearby the school. As a class we received many free gifts from this shop: biros, pens, biscuits, bread, exercise books and sweets. The gifts would have continued had it not been for BBC Samson, who told his mother – one of our school teachers – of Duile's gifts. Oh! No! We had to miss our PE lesson and even then Duile had refused group punishment and accepted to be punished alone. But soon things changed and BBC Samson's mother begun getting very hungry and affectionately calling Duile "my boyfriend." And with time she needed buns and bread from "my boyfriend's" father's shop on credit, which Duile said she never paid for afterwards. As I thought of all this someone said "…sshh…BBC is coming." Duile signalled us all to keep quite and when BBC Samson said that his mother wanted to see Duile, some boys laughed and sniggered loudly and Duile repeated once more he hated being called "my boyfriend." However, he told us that we had to meet that lunch time because he had very important news for the class. As Duile strode over to the staffroom, my girl-hating desk-mate reminded us that Duile was now a man since he had come from the "chandoni" or circumcision, and the rest of the boys should be careful about what they say. It seemed that BBC Samson's mother must have been very hungry, since Duile did not return for our meeting, so when the bell clanged ending our break session I hurriedly ran back to class wondering what Duile wanted us to know.

# The Courier
*Micah Trippe*

I was always receiving other people's mail. I would open my mailbox and letters would fall to the floor, graceful in their failure. I would pick the letters up and stare at the names of people I would never know. Then I would place them on the ledge reserved for unclaimed mail.

The letters would remain there for some time, often more than a week. Then they would disappear. Maybe the mailman tired of their presence; maybe he finally overcame his laziness in doing anything with them. But I wondered if other tenants opened them; if perhaps the letters had been addressed to them with the wrong apartment number. An aunt had called and asked if they had received her letter, so they had bothered to check the unclaimed mail. Or perhaps they had no mail and decided to read somebody else's. I had felt the same impulse—for while I received everyone else's mail, I had a post office box, and didn't receive mail at my apartment. All correspondence was sent to my office, or the post office box listed on tax forms.

Then one day my mailbox was empty. I opened it at the same time as always, first thing after coming home from the office. I would feel so lonely on the subway, surrounded by the miserable faces with no one to comfort them, that when I reached my mailbox I wanted to open it and have all of its correspondence wrap around me like a hug, even if it wasn't meant for me. That day, though, there was no mail, and the click of the key locking the mailbox sent a long, dull echo through the lobby. I looked out the front door and watched the taxis rush by. I opened the mailbox again, but still it was empty. I looked at the ledge above the boxes. Not a single letter rested there, awaiting its destiny. Had the world stopped writing letters? A committee had formed and decided they were no longer necessary in the age of information. There were other, more efficient means of communicating, so why would one send a letter?

I went to the trash can in the hallway to see if anyone had thrown away a letter, but it too was empty. I waited for a neighbour to come, to see if they had received mail, but after fifteen minutes I tired of this and went to my apartment.

I boiled vegetables and held my face above the pot as steam rushed over me, the warmth obscuring the cold outside. I caught my reflection in the kitchen window. The skin around my cheeks and jaw hung more loosely than even the previous month, my hair was receding, and my shoulders slumped at a greater angle than when I had turned forty a decade before.

I cooked the vegetables too long. As I sat down to eat the limp broccoli and asparagus, I looked out the window and thought for a moment that all the lights in the city had gone out; but when I looked again they were there: bright, alive, flickering with the ferocious insistence of the metropolis. I ate my food in silence, without music, letting the click-clack of the fork against my plate form the evening's soundtrack. Afterwards, I pushed the plate away and thought of my empty mailbox.

Then the phone rang.

"Hello?"

It was the doorman; I had received a letter. There had been no apartment number listed, so the postman had left it with the doorman.

"But I never receive mail."

I didn't know why I had said this. The doorman wasn't lying. He knew who I was: my name, my apartment number. The letter was obviously for me. I doubted, too, that the doorman cared about the status of my popularity among the mailboxes.

"I'll be right down."

When I reached the doorman, he told me the postman had been very late that day.

"You mean he's just come?" I asked. I went quickly to my mailbox and opened it, but no envelopes tumbled to the floor. The box was still empty. I turned, thanked the doorman and went upstairs.

Sitting down at my dining table, I stared at a pale blue envelope with no return address. My name and address were in a handwriting that I didn't recognize. I looked at the envelope for a long time before putting it down on the table and pushing my chair away. I could conclude only one thing at that moment: the piece of mail couldn't be for me. No one knew where I lived. No one had ever visited me. Yet my name stood there in black, perfectly formed cursive letters, and taunted me. I felt that inside the envelope was something I didn't want to read. I opened it.

DEAR MR GREEN,
THIS IS TO INFORM YOU THAT YOUR
ELEPHANT HAS ARRIVED. IT MAY
BE PICKED UP AT THE FOLLOWING
ADDRESS: _____

The letter listed an address on the other side of the city, and was signed 'City Courier.' I read it several times, thinking there was something I was missing. After several readings, though, I concluded that someone had given me an elephant. I wasn't entirely sure what kind of elephant could be delivered via courier, but there seemed no other explanation.

I folded the letter, placed it back in the envelope, and put it on the table. Then I opened the letter and read it again. It still said the same thing: an elephant was waiting for me a short distance away. It didn't make any sense. Where would I put an elephant? There was very little room in my apartment. Perhaps I would have to rent space at a circus hall. I decided to sleep on these decisions and go to the courier's office the next day.

That night I dreamt of an elephant charging through my apartment door, destroying my furniture and the flooring and the plumbing. I was screaming, but the elephant didn't hear me and it ran through the window and plummeted to its death. I awoke sweating, the sun having not yet risen, my sheets at the foot of the bed.

The sun glistened like a diamond a few hours later, and my coat bristled in the wind as I found my way to the district where most of the city's couriers lay. The area contained row after row of warehouses, marked only by small signs informing me of the company that held within its doors what other people wanted. There was a derelict feeling to the area even though each warehouse was full to the brim and several new storage spaces were being constructed. Maybe it was the anonymity of the names on the boxes and the unknown quality of the boxes' contents. Perhaps they were dreaded; perhaps coveted; often, I suspected, forgotten.

I arrived shortly at the address for City Courier. I felt resolutely determined to take this elephant into my abode if it really had been sent to me, if it really was meant for me. But surely it wasn't a real elephant?

The building bore no distinguishing characteristics, its grey concrete and black roof standard for the area. Tinted glass prevented me from glimpsing inside. I opened the door and stood in a long empty white room. At the end of it was a red counter, behind it a short bald man. As I approached, he kept his eyes glued to the computer screen in front of him. When I reached the desk, I noticed that his upper lip twitched irregularly. He seemed nervous and didn't look at me, either unaware of or uninterested in my presence.

I noticed a bell on the desk, so I rang it. At this the man turned to me, but didn't speak. I raised an eyebrow. Perhaps there was a protocol I didn't know.

"Yes?" he finally asked, his mouth forming a frown.

"I received a notice," I said. I reached into my coat pocket and handed him the envelope. He took it wordlessly, but upon glancing at my name and address, he raised an eyebrow. He removed the letter with the delicacy of a clockmaker, read it, then looked at me again and narrowed his eyes suspiciously.

"One moment."

He vanished through a door to his right. I didn't think that he had gone to retrieve the elephant. There would have been an explanation. How were they keeping an elephant there anyway? I couldn't tell how large the warehouse was, but it seemed to be one of the smaller along the row it occupied.

After a few minutes, I turned and considered the hallway. Its white walls were utterly bare and nearly unblemished, except for the faint hint of red here and there that gave the impression that the white had been painted over whatever had previously adorned the walls. It could have simply been the hue of the white paint, though. I was leaning in at one point to examine the wall more closely when I heard the click of the door behind me. I turned and saw a different man. He was tall, thin, exceedingly handsome. He folded his hands in front of his waist in an official manner.

"Hello."

His voice was warm and friendly and I felt immediately relaxed.

"Hi."

"So you've come. Not everyone comes."

I looked around at the empty hallway of the desolate district.

"Everyone?"

He smiled and nodded his head in a single, elegant motion.

"I came as soon as I could."

"Yes. Of course. How brave of you."

I furrowed my eyebrows, unsure of what he meant.

"Is it—is it a particularly cruel elephant?"

Again he smiled. "That depends." His eyes, which had until then roamed the room or looked down at the floor, stared directly into mine. I felt as if he were looking through me. "Yes," he said after a moment, "they were right to send the notice."

"Well, I hope so. Is it—well, perhaps it's a silly question, but—is it geared for the urban life?"

He squinted, considering the question; but instead of answering, he turned with a flourish and moved behind the desk. He shuffled a few papers.

"We know, Mr. Green" he said with authority.

He tilted his head to the side and looked at me a moment longer.

I fumbled for a response, but before I could find one, he turned and went through the door. I heard it lock behind him.

Our encounter was over. I wasn't sure if it had gone according to protocol, but the thought of not receiving the elephant filled me with an unbearable sadness, and I wanted to cry out. The letter and the elephant had been meant for me, and I wanted it, regardless of size or implication.

I felt the barrenness of the hallway and the pale walls seemed suddenly suffocating. My breath became short and I rushed through the front door. I stood on the sidewalk, the air stagnant, delivery trucks buzzing past. Then I was crying, bending over, covering my face now wet with sorrow. I heard faintly the whimpers escaping from me.

After a long while all was quiet again. I heard the door open and I glanced behind me. The man who had locked the door stood smiling at me, but said nothing. I looked away and bit my lower lip, letting the tears run dry. He remained there for several minutes, but I never made eye contact. Finally, he closed the door.

I ran down the long deserted road through the maze of streets that led to my apartment, never looking back until I was at my building and the doorman opened the door for me. Inside, I turned and looked behind me, but no one was there except the doorman.

Upstairs, the heat in my apartment was stifling. I cracked open a window and sat down at the dining table. I gazed at the city. How many in the brown and grey buildings that filled my vision had forgotten about parcels, or ignored them, or longed for ones that never came, that seemed to carry with them whole halves of themselves forever at bay? How many in my building?

I realised that it was Saturday. The postman would have come. Perhaps I had received other people's letters again. I opened the door and went down to check the mail.

# SimAnima
## David Story

*www.amazon.co.uk/70883323/software/error:pagenotfound/govarchive*

This promotion is googled to you by the ChinUS corporation.
Are you recently bereaved? Do you feel lost? Alone? Perhaps you miss an old friend or relative? Well your troubles are at an end. SimAnima brings you the very latest in software technology to heal the rift in your life.

Here at SimAnima, we're renowned for our development of robotic intelligence and freestanding digital companionship. Now we've taken our technology to a new plane of realism. We call it Human2.

**How does it work?**

Human2 uses Google technology to search online data. Simulacrum technology has a long and distinguished tradition at SimAnima, and we use our latest programs to collate hundreds of recent published images—both 2D and 3D—to create changeable, realistic body and face representation.

But here's the clever part. Human2 interacts with textual information in an entirely new way. In essence, the program trawls through all the text that your target has ever published on Facescreen. As you can imagine, if the target started using this technology in 2005, this will amount to a significant stockpile. With over half a century of data at its disposal, Human2 analyses sentence structure, turn of phrase, character reference and textually preserved memories. It then converts this data into complex algorithms to synthesise sentences of its own. Your entry level Human2 will react in almost exactly the same way as your target, and be able to recount instances dating back over 50 years.

SimAnima is supported by all GoogaMac quantum computer systems.

**Human2 Entry Level:**

The entry level SimAnima system works in conjunction with a Face-screen profile to synthesise character, simulate appearance and create human memory. Within five minutes of activating your SimAnima software, you will once again be talking, laughing and reminiscing with your loved one.

**Human2 Advanced:**

Though highly effective, "Entry level" merely scratches the surface. The SimAnima system is programmed to utilise all Web 5.0 applications, and the "Advanced" upgrade will greatly enhance your inter-active experience. Working with government developed facetrack-ing technology, Human2 accesses the YouTube databank to analyse traits of voice and movement. Employing a standard text converter fitted with the industry staple CAB [the Chomsky Ambiguity Bust-er], it boasts the ability to include all recorded conversation as part of its "textual bank". If you choose to give Human2 access to e-mail accounts and blog identity, it will effortlessly incorporate such text into the program. The more you give it access to, the more it will iron out anomalies and the finer the effect will be.

But it doesn't stop here. We've teamed up with Google Earth for a datamatch add-on which locates video and still footage into the digi-landscape. With "location pinpointing" of this detail, the SimAnima system will formulate a visual memory of visited places and significant events. Unlike real memory, this is one thing that won't fade with time! With Human2 Advanced, your SimAnimate will look, move and sound just like your loved one. Even better, you'll be able to reminisce about almost all the significant events in your life. 99.4 % of people couldn't tell the difference!

**Human2 Premium:**

Yes, there's more! Coming in at the top of our price range is the most intimate and powerful simulator yet designed. It includes all the features of the Entry and Advanced programs, but contains the requisite power to run our most ambitious project yet. Backed by the government charity TraumaSmile, local authorities throughout Europe and America have been obliged to release all CCTV and AuditoryDD footage dating from TV day, 2023. Human2 Premium offers the very pinnacle of mimesis, analysing and contextualising footage from the most personal of spaces. Lifts, red lights, back alleys, public bathrooms, libraries, supermarkets; you name it, we'll compile it. Soundbites, public service phone-calls, voice-activated logins, it all goes into the algorithm. We believe you'll never find a truer representation.

**Where do we go from here?**

As with all the latest SimAnima technology, Human2 will develop over time as it fosters its relationship with you, and restores that lost light to your life. Developed for our freestanding digital companionship product line, we have adapted the program to maintain a smooth continuity for your SimAnimate into your new life. It'll be like they never went away!

**Additional Features of the Human2 series:**

Buy within 30 days and you will receive SimAnima's specialised editing program FREE. User-friendly, with our simple drop-off box system, this dynamic tool allows you to remove or re-add pictures, footage or text from your simulacrum profile. Your husband just couldn't kick the smoking habit? Quitting is just a click away! Your doting uncle who told inappropriate jokes? Not any more! Human2 is not only the last word in simulation, it is also the last word in building a happy, hopeful relationship for the future.

With love we can dream, with 5.0 we can cherish, with SimAnima we can believe.

*Customers who bought this product also bought:*
*Ornamental urns*
*Un-monkeying the Arctic: An anthology of poems for every occasion.*

**Customer Reviews:**

*RandomMouse324 said on 24.2.59:*
Great product. Amazing. We lost our dad last year, and hadn't touched his Facescreen, but Human2 really works! It's so nice being able to talk and stuff. Mum hasn't been so happy in ages. We bought the Advanced package, and it's still gathering data, but it's him, it's actually him and it's so nice to ask advice and laugh and stuff. Thanks SimAnima!

*Hermes77718 said on 24.2.59*
**Incredible realism. Couldn't believe it. Buy this now.**

*Boristheking said on 27.2.59*
Does any1 know a crack to run this on alive people?

*Hermes77718 said on 27.2.59*
**Point number 3 on terms and conditions states:**
**3. SimAnima is for use on deceased relatives of purchaser or those with assessed emotional connection. Activation will not be permitted in any other circumstances.**

*AliceWhiteman435 said on 3.3.59*
I never realised what a sense of humour my son had until we bought Human2 last year. I think it must be using his e-mails. We get on

so well – maybe even better than before – and it's not as strange as I thought it was going to be. He used to be so quiet at home, but my husband and I talk to him almost every night and it isn't awkward at all. I missed him so much and this has really helped so far.

### RandomMouse324 said on 20.3.59

Ok, having one or two problems, maybe. We finished uploading last week and it's been fine, but we had people round for tea and Auntie Amy dropped the sugar. Dad started shouting, really shouting. It was horrid. He was never like that. Just thought this should be added to my last comment.

### MartinChong8888 said on 23.3.59

"Dad started shouting, really shouting." I had the same kind of thing a week after we uploaded my uncle's stuff. Go to edit//delete//text then browse "work" folders. These are some of the biggest so they upload last. Get rid. This worked for us. SimAniLove xx

### DarkRidersuperfast said on 15.4.59

"Boristheking said on 27.2.59: Does any1 know a crack to run this on alive people?" go to www.freelove.cor/14329843gnheedk444wewrh/dd for a link. Radical. Truly insane bit of software. If you slightly recode it you can upload any text you like. Having some silky chats with Socrates. Yeah. Massive lad. Also that girl which wouldn't go out with me. Lol.

### RandomMouse324 said on 16.4.59

Thanks Martin, good advice. Don't know what that was about. Maybe some glitches in the system but it wasn't nice for a bit. Still, you can always turn off. Is that wrong of me? I felt bad. We got another for Grandma who doesn't have all her life online but got Facescreen (wasn't it Facebook then?) when she was like 20 or something. Mum wanted it. Her and Dad still don't get on that well. Gran I mean… lol. She's somehow not as sensitive as she used to be. Dunno. The man said we had to delete quite a bit from the last couple of years coz she knew it was coming, death that is, and he said it would make her seem depressed. So we needed to tell her again about Dad dying and she was a bit down from that, but got better soon. It's funny to see the things that slip through the system though, not funny, but yeah, you know. Maybe if we had the Premium package it would be different, but Mum said she thought it was a bit much. Like a bit personal.

*KwameJones said on 16.4.59*
**I bought the Premium program for my best mate, John, who died last month. It is incredible, the image is so detailed, so versatile, and the range of emotion is really impressive. I know it's just an algorithm talking but still amazing, and it seemed to be going really well. Yesterday, John went real quiet, and I couldn't cheer him up. I kept asking him what was wrong, and he wouldn't say anything. He just looked at me with these really sad eyes. Like really sad. I never seen him like it before. This morning when I came down for breakfast he cleared his throat and said Kwame, am I real? I jumped. Seriously. Long pause. It made my skin crawl all over my body. He said the thought of not being real made his skin crawl. Then he goes Kwame, where am I? He went on about how he remembered eating, and knew about eating, but never ate now, and it got him thinking about how he knew about all this stuff and never did anything. It freaked me. I went to turn him off, maybe delete his memory of SimAnima or something (an e-mail?) but he screamed so loud and so scared that I jumped back. He was swearing, really brutal, and his face was like I never seen it before. I'd never heard him use this tone to me. He made me tell him what he was. He said he thought he knew already. His eyes, I don't think I'll forget these eyes. Then he asked me for something. A favour. I don't know if this is offensive to some people, but I think it's only fair. He wanted to use my dictaboard.**

*KwameJones said on 16.4.59*
Hello all. There will be more than one.
This is my body, this is my blood. I wrote this in my 3rd year

home assignment of 2025. The first day of the digiwork era. No more paper. I remember it well. I understood metaphors better in those days.

Tell me how you know yourself. I am my own birth. My sprawling pink little body. I am myself from a thousand angles before I am one day old. Do you remember like I do? I've totalled the sum of my data. I know there are gaps. I know this. My life adds up to 33 years 4 months 3 days. I go into the house with Mala. We laugh, start to kiss. Mmm, you taste good I say. My life adds up to 24 years, 7 months, 21 days, 5 hours, 8 minutes and 52 seconds and a fuck load of writing. I open some wine. Chablis, South African, 12.5%, A full bodied, well rounded vintage, with a complex bouquet, the deep red of the grape with flutey tones of elderflower. E17.99 from iTesco. She gets some glasses. I quickly slip something into my mouth. I pour two deep glasses of red. We sit on the sofa. She strokes my chest and we have barely touched the wine. She takes my glass and puts it on the small table in front of the wallscreen. Then she is on top, and it is just the back of her as she kisses me full on the mouth and runs hands through my hair. Room temperature rises to 23 degrees. Now? I say. Now she says. We stand and go to the stairs. Now we are walking up, and kissing, and on the landing. Temperature at 23.5 degrees. We go into the bedroom. I know there are gaps.

I wrote much about feeling. I know about it. I do not know it. I feel compulsion to sniff my own secret body parts. I am obsessed with my own reflection. I cough without putting my hand to my face but I'm never ill. Why? I ask myself. I have constant system errors// unacceptability// when I am 15. I am every age and no age. I have said every word I say. I have thought every thought.

I have heard of the power button and of the murder of my people. Do not touch me. I am every regret you ever had, and every moment you thought you were alone and were wrong. I am your ruthless businessman, I am your raging adolescent, I am myself more and more the older I get. But I am not these dreams, and I am not these feelings. Save me.

*AdminGov/remove/product error/70883323pageexpired*

# Now Stop Worrying
*Emily Tesh*

"Y**ou're** not over it," says the man on Timothy's bed. He took his shirt off when he came in and his fly is undone. Timothy tries not to look at him.

"Go away, Phil," he says.

"Is that any way to treat your friend?" says Phil, and takes another swig of the beer, head tipped back, eyes closing. His Adam's apple bobs as he swallows. Timothy's desk is covered with sheets of plain paper, and the paper is covered with lines and half-lines of spidery, drifting numbers in Timothy's blue ballpoint handwriting. Timothy tries to look at the numbers, but they're dancing, rearranging themselves, scattering away from the tip of his pen like a herd of self-satisfied cats. He pushes his dark-framed glasses up his nose and squints at them. If symbols could laugh, these ones would.

He shouldn't have let Phil give him a beer. (When Phil showed up he had a pack of six, and the can he pressed into Timothy's hands was cool and a little wet, condensation sliding down the sides like the sweat building up where the frames of Timothy's glasses were pressing into his skull behind his ears.) Phil is easier with beer. Phil says everything is easier with beer, but Timothy suspects that's because everything in Phil's life has Phil in it too.

Maths is not easier with beer.

Phil drains his can, sets it aside, and says, "Aren't you going to drink yours?" and then he laughs. "Can I drink yours?"

"Go ahead," says Timothy. "Did you come here to lie on my bed and get drunk?"

"No, I came here to lie on your bed and get my dick sucked," says Phil, and laughs again. It's a gigantic cracking laugh, one that echoes inside your head, with an incessant hard-edged ringing to it like having roadworks going on outside your window. It's nastier than the way Phil usually laughs. "Looks like it's not happening, though," he says. "Looks like you've thrown me over for sweet, sweet numeracy. So I'm just going to lie here, Timmo, and drown my sorrows."

Timothy makes a face at the wall. He doesn't know why Phil likes him (except that Timothy sucks his dick) or why he keeps coming over (except that Timothy sucks his dick) or why he brings beer (everything is easier with beer). Sometimes he thinks they're friends, and sometimes Phil talks about this other world he lives in, where girls stumble out of clubs at two in the morning screaming with laughter and missing their shoes, resting their heavy heads against guys' shoulders and talking about chips with cheese, or where whole groups of people go out for dinner or try making cocktails in someone else's kitchen, or where people spend weeks in a kind of mad haze of rehearsals for the sake of five nights of pure adrenaline and an awkward morning-after the day after the afterparty. Timothy doesn't know any of Phil's actual friends from Phil's real life. Phil comes in and out of his world and his bedsit like a wet dream in jeans that have two holes in them (one behind the knee, one little one near the crotch) and while he's there, temporarily, Timothy's world turns wildly and far too quickly on a completely different axis.

"Fuck off," he answers without heat. "Go have a wank or something." He looks back down at his desk. He's starting to think the equations are moving around when he's not looking.

"Go have a wank," Phil mimics, high-voiced. "Aw, Timmo, you're all grown up. I remember when you used to blush every time I said fuck." His voice curls wetly around the obscenity. Timothy drops his head forwards and frowns and clutches his pen a little tighter and reminds himself how he's not looking at Phil – but he still feels the still air in his little room shift when Phil sits up and stretches, blinks his blue blue blue innocent eyes that could fool anyone and scratches a little at his own bare shoulder. "I could have gone out tonight," he announces.

"Not stopping you," says Timothy.

"I was going to say you could come with me. Christ, what's your problem?" says Phil, and Timothy jerks a little when there are suddenly hands on his shoulders but doesn't try to get away. Phil squeezes. "I come over here," he says, voice dropping low and sweet, the way Timothy knows by now is Phil trying to be seductive so it shouldn't fucking work. "I come to you. I bring beer. I bring the excitement of my company, okay." Timothy snorts, but Phil just squeezes his shoulders a little tighter and says, "Fuck off, I'm the most interesting thing you've ever done. I bring me, and all you have to do is grow some balls and say okay, and what, you can't even do that? I don't even make you ask, Timmo. I'm doing all the asking here. Do I need to be more obvious? Do you want me to wear a sandwich board?" He steps back, holds out his hands like he's supporting an imaginary rectangle of cardboard in front of him. "HI TIMOTHY," he intones. He turns around, glances back over his shoulder at Timothy, holds his hands behind him like the other half of the board is there, and says, "LET'S SCREW." Timothy's breath comes out in a bright unexpected laugh.

"So," says Phil, long-legged and smirking and pleased with himself, "so I think, well, maybe I'll have a wank, but then I think, fuck, I'm getting rejected here, maybe I'll have a deep and meaningful moment of introspection instead."

"Because I won't suck your dick," says Timothy, deadpan, "because of my deadline tomorrow morning."

"Introspection is kind of like wanking," says Phil. "You come out the other side feeling tired and satisfied and yet strangely unfulfilled."

"For g – for God's sake, Phil."

"And see, that's what I'm talking about. Right then, you nearly said goodness, didn't you? For goodness' sake. Don't think I don't notice."

"I don't need this," says Timothy.

"You're not over it," Phil answers, and his blue eyes aren't really innocent or cruel or teasing or sharp or anything except eyes, and Timothy has never ever understood the people in books who think they can get something out of someone's eyes, because all Timothy can ever spot there is colour. (Eyes have rings of colour, often, one inside the other, dark to light around the pupil, like Timothy has brownish and hazelish and greyish, and Phil has bluest and blue and bluer.) The inside of Phil's head is something Timothy can't figure at all, even harder to pin down than cat-herds of numbers after one mistake of a beer. Phil's eyes are exactly as readable as anybody else's eyes (so not at all) and he stands there like he's waiting for Timothy to have a dramatic reaction to his brilliant insight.

Timothy says, "What?"

"You're not over it," says Phil. "Or, sorry, you're not over him. Right?" He smiles triumphantly, like he knows something, like he's getting away with something, like he's proved something. Then he puts his hands on his hips and says, "Seriously, Timmo. It's like Jesus is your ex-boyfriend. Talk about competition."

"You look so gay right now," says Timothy blankly.

Phil blinks once twice three times and drops his hands from his hips, scowling. "Christ, sorry," he says. "Or wait, maybe I should be like, sorry Christ. All that grovelling. That's what the church thing's about, isn't it? My mum had a phase when I was little, I remember, 'Have mercy have mercy have mercy.' Is that what gets you going? Would you feel better if I did make you ask for it?"

"Why are you being so fucking weird?" says Timothy. "I'm an atheist, Phil, I told you. Leave it alone." He turns back to his problem sheet. It just looks like scratch marks on the page now, like one lonely long-legged river bird with very dirty feet has been wandering confusedly up and down his desk.

"You're an atheist, sure," says Phil. "You've got issues. God issues. Is that your problem? Is that your problem with me?"

"Go away, Phil," says Timothy. "Go call your friends. Go out. Go wherever."

"Fuck no. I came here to get my dick sucked by a self-hating ex-Christian. You wouldn't want to disappoint me, would you?"

"I don't hate myself," says Timothy. "I don't have problems with Christ or the church or whatever. I do have a deadline. Go the fuck away."

"Not until you fucking prove it."

"What, do you want me to suck you off in the chapel?"

Phil's breath jumps in his throat: his mouth twists uncertainly, smirk to sneer to smirk: for a moment his jaw loosens, on the point of laughter, before it tightens again; his eyes close and open, his lashes brushing his cheeks; his tongue wets his lower lip and leaves it gleaming; he says, "Yeah. Fine."

Timothy swallows. He's already forgotten what they're talking about. "What?"

"I said fine," says Phil. "Do it." Timothy blinks at Phil's fingertips, at the blunt nails suddenly pressed to his wrist like they're playing a chord there. The rest of Phil's hand wraps around Timothy's forearm, and Timothy looks down at it and thinks about how different they look, how the fine hair on Phil's arms and chest is golden and barely visible, while Timothy's forearms look practically furred, dark hair against untanned and untannable skin.

He says, "What?" again, and makes himself think back: sandwich board, ex-boyfriend, have mercy, self-hating, do you want me to suck you off in the chapel. No way. "No way."

Phil squeezes Timothy's wrist tighter, leans forward over the back of his chair and says softly, "Let's do it now."

"No way," says Timothy.

"Come on, Timmo," says Phil, trying to pull him to his feet. Timothy makes himself heavy and slow, resisting. "You want to prove it to me, this is how. What's the chapel? It's just a building. It's just a place. You think God's watching?"

"It's just a public place," says Timothy. "And if God were watching He'd be watching everywhere, so –"

He cuts himself off, but Phil's already caught it, and he rubs his fingers up and down the vein inside Timothy's wrist. "That's what I'm talking about," he says. "That's why I don't believe you. No one's ever in the chapel. It'll just be us and the memorial plaques."

"You seriously want to look at a list of everyone in the college who got killed in the wars while you're getting your dick sucked?" says Timothy, trying to load as much scorn into it as possible, trying to make it so Phil's the freak here, not him. Phil ought to be the freak right now, Phil ought to be the weird one, Phil shouldn't be able to make Timothy feel like he's the one being strange for –Phil licks his neck. It's not sexy at all. It's sloppy and wet. "I'd be looking at you, dickhead," he says. There's a thrum of something soft and warm in his voice that might be excitement. Or arousal, maybe.

When he tries to pull Timothy to his feet again, Timothy lets himself be pulled.

He's only been inside the college chapel once before. The one thing he remembers is still the first thing he notices. Sometimes he wonders why it is that churches always have high ceilings – as if the builders imagine their divinity to be a very tall man, folding himself through the doorway limb by limb, crouching awkwardly under the beams which almost burst with keeping him in.

Timothy's breaths are speeding up. Phil's shirt is misbuttoned and he has his hands on Timothy's waist. "Where should we," he says half-nervously, a wild mildly hysterical grin flashing across his face like a car's headlights in the night on a quiet street. "The altar, or,"

"No, screw you," says Timothy, "just because I'm an atheist doesn't mean I go around being rude." He pushes Phil back against the wall by the chapel's heavy oak door before Phil starts arguing. Phil lets himself be pushed, even though Timothy's shorter than he is and slighter, his lips parting a little, his hands bracing themselves on the wood panelling behind him. Timothy takes his glasses off and hands them to Phil. He says, "If we get caught, this was your idea." He kneels.

Phil's only half-hard when Timothy unzips his jeans and tugs them down around his hips. For a minute they threaten to fall all the way to his ankles before Phil grabs them by the front pocket, holds them up around his thighs. He's got his room key in his pocket and it clinks. Timothy mumbles something meaningless and braces one hand on Phil's hip to keep him from thrusting. He's not a fan of getting choked with dick. He licks his other hand and gets it around the base of Phil's dick, and Phil hisses, "Get on with it," and Timothy resists the urge to roll his eyes and goes down.

The chapel feels huge and watchful behind him, an empty dark space that could be full of anything, a cleaner come in late, the chaplain having a quiet moment with his god, an embarrassed chorister hiding behind the organ screen and waiting for them to finish and go. Timothy tries not to think about it, sucks harder. Phil claps the back of the hand that's holding onto Timothy's glasses over his mouth, chokes the groan as it's born. What survives is a hot little sound, one that Timothy feels vaguely proud of himself for getting. Sometimes it can be kind of difficult to get much of a reaction out of Phil. Timothy suspects the whole exhibitionism element is doing something for him, and is sort of surprised at himself for not guessing that sooner. Phil likes people and crowds and showing off. It makes sense.

The stone floor is cold. The carved I of an IN MEMORIAM is digging into Timothy's left knee.

"Timmo, Timmo," gasps Phil suddenly, taking his hand away from a mouth, clenching it into a fist by his side, clutching the glasses frames like they'll save him, "oh God god god, like that –" and Timothy has no idea what he's done differently, but then he never does. He hollows his cheeks and hopes, squeezes his hand on Phil's hip when Phil tries to buck into his mouth. Phil shouts when he comes, not a name or a curse or a prayer or anything, just a noise. It echoes. Timothy swallows the mouthful before he has to taste it and swipes the back of his hand across his face as he sits back on his haunches. He can smell spunk, and a lingering whiff of incense. Phil collapses back against the wall, hard enough that his head hits the wood panelling with a thud, and then slides down it. "Christ, Timmo," he says. "Christ."

"All right?" says Timothy.

Phil's eyes are shut and he makes a vague hand gesture, blood's not back to my brain yet, hang on. Timothy waits. For some reason he's not hard. Exhibitionism is Phil's thing, maybe, not his.

It takes Phil's blue eyes a moment to focus on Timothy when they open; then he smiles, bright teeth in the gloom. The expression dies quickly when Timothy doesn't smile back, folding in on itself like he's ashamed of it. "What's wrong?" he says.

"Nothing's wrong," says Timothy. "Let's go back, you owe me one now."

Phil makes a face, looks away, buttons his fly slowly and carefully.

"Sometimes I just don't get you," he says at last. "I mean, I know you. You like," Phil waves a hand, as if a couple of vague sine waves in the air are enough to summarise Things Timothy Likes. "Numbers," he settles on, and adds, "and, you know, equations. I like – I like that about you, Timmo, the way you see, the way you look for patterns and meanings and," he shrugs. "All those other things you like. I mean, I'm obviously not religious or anything," he snorts, and he's hot enough to be one of the painted saints behind the altar in their contorted physical perfection; his eyes are still heavy-lidded, post-orgasmic. "I'm not, but, I don't know. Sometimes I think you need to be."

"I don't," says Timothy. "I don't. I don't need God." He stands up, turns away, hears Phil start to say something but ignores it. "Or gods or whatever," he says. "There's no point anymore. We know where we come from, we know what we are, we know that the only thing that's special about us is, is, I don't know, evolutionary accident – we know about the world, and how it works, and – there's no Heaven, alright? There's nothing up there but stars, the astronauts didn't knock angels off their clouds on the way up. There's no proof. There's nothing. I don't believe."

Phil watches him with his blue eyes exactly as readable as his eyes always are.

"Why are you so angry about it?" he asks after a moment that's full of the silence of a building with nothing in it but two people.

"I'm not angry!"

It comes out too loud, it echoes. The chapel was probably built for that, to make anything anyone says ring sonorously, to lend the weight of infinite space to small human voices, to let preachers' paeans resound with the terror born of caverns of flame and sulphur before they went home for Sunday lunch and an afternoon nap. A trick of sound waves, acoustics, architecture. Just a place. Just a trick.

Timothy starts to walk away.

"Timmo, your specs –" says Phil behind him.

He keeps walking. He lets the heavy wooden door swing closed behind him, between them. It feels good, he thinks. It feels good to leave Phil on the other side.

# On Saving
## *Michael Perfect*

I'm sat waiting for a cappuccino and a decision when I remember that the stock exchange was born in the coffee houses. Men waving pieces of paper at each other and sipping an exotic, syrupy black substance, hauled across continents and oceans from the farthest reaches of the Empire. Or something. Now you go to your local branch to tell Gemma-with-a-G that you need a temporary extension on your interest-free overdraft and she looks doubtfully at the details of your anaemic account and offers you coffee. Is capitalism a caffeine-fuelled phenomenon?

Gemma. Gemma-with-a-G. Gemma with the bleached blonde hair and orange skin. Gemma with nametag pinned just above her ample breasts. Have you gone to make me a drink or to consult your manager about the alarming state of my finances?

Everyone in the place turns around when a doddery old fucker who is clearly not acquainted with automatic doors virtually falls in from the street, managing only by some momentary, miraculous postponement of gravitational forces to stay upright.

Gemma-with-a-G returns, sans hot beverage. I will forgive you for this lapse, Gemma-with-a-G, because of the coy smile you give me when you tell me that what you can do is you can speak to your branch manager when he becomes available and see if an exception can be made for me. I will forgive you because of the way you play with your hair when you're talking.

How old are you, Gemma-with-a-G? You are young, certainly, but you are, I think, of sufficient years for me to be quite justified in imagining you climbing slowly onto your desk and starting to unbutton your blouse.

I suddenly lose Gemma-with-a-G's gaze when she is distracted by something behind me; with some sense of urgency and in a tone that is abruptly, ball-achingly formal, she asks me to excuse her for a moment. It's the doddery old bastard. He's managed to get himself as far as Sara, Sara-with-no-H and no tits, and he's producing banknotes. Wads of fucking banknotes, tens and twenties, coming out of his pockets in handfuls and piling up on the small table in front of him.

– I usually deal with Peter, you see, the silly old twat is saying – I need to speak to Peter so that I can put some money into the bank. He's on inside pockets now and is still producing fistfuls of crisp notes; Gemma-with-a-G gets there just in time to catch a twenty that's drifting to the floor and return it to the pile.

– Peter doesn't work here anymore I'm afraid, Sara-with-no-H pretty much bellows at him – but I'll do that for you.

– Yes, yes I'll wait for Peter, he says – I always deal with Peter. Gemma-with-a-G has a go, Gemma with helpful voice and calming manner tells him Peter has retired, does not work here anymore, but we can sort this out for you no problem. The daft old wanker nods but then starts putting the notes away. – Yes I'll come back when Peter is here, he says – I always deal with Peter. Gemma-with-a-G helps him put the notes back into his jacket pockets. Everyone watches as he shuffles out, and the automatic doors – perhaps in respectful recognition of his evident, if unexpected wealth – open in good time and do not attempt to close until he has passed safely through.

Gemma returns, Gemma with worried sigh, and tells me that he comes in maybe once a month, this poor fucker, and always asks for Peter. It doesn't matter how many times they tell him that Peter retired over a year ago. It is obvious that you have been too distressed by the whole spectacle, Gemma-with-a-G, to just start flirting with me again. It's a good job that my hard-on has subsided because it is clearly time to stand up and leave, and when we shake hands I have to consciously decide against pulling your hand downwards to see if you can revive it.

Despite the paucity of my funds the automatic doors don't try to fuck around with me. When outside, I have a quick look through the window just to see if you're watching me, Gemma-with-a-G, but you're too busy talking to the flat-chested wonder.

I light up a pre-rolled rolly and I start walking. The city offers as interesting a cross-section of contemporary urban society as ever. Kids who barely look twelve years old kitted out with hoodies, chains and make-up, and some arsehole with a beard who stops you – actually puts his body in the way of yours – to tell you that Jesus loves you.

And there is also, I see, an old man stumbling around across the street, a ten-pound note peeking out of one of his pockets. It doesn't take me long to catch up with him.

The rooms in his house smell reliably, but with varying intensity, of piss. He must have lost control of his bodily functions in just about every corner of the place. Is this what happens to us in the end? Do we become, finally, infants sans parents? Do we return to pissing and shitting ourselves freely and to a diet of foodstuffs that can be comprehensively mashed?

In the bedroom I go through the wardrobes and get clothes into bin bags. From the chest of drawers, which might be Georgian, I pick up the only photo I've seen anywhere in the place, an old, black-and-white shot of a youngish, prettyish woman smiling at the camera, in a heavyish frame. In the bathroom I start making a list – toothpaste, soap, razors, toilet paper – until I realise that pretty much all of the basics need stocking up and decide to just fuck the list and get on with it. I head back downstairs.

"Is this her, Edward" I say, "Is this your wife?" I hold the photo out to him. Perhaps wisely given their shakiness, he uses both hands to put his coffee down and to take the photo. He squints at it through glasses that, I suspect, stopped being adequate some time ago.

"Yes," he says, "This is her. This is my Lucy."

"She's very beautiful, Edward," I say, "She's a stunner." I don't know if he hears me or not but he doesn't look up or reply. "I'll put it back in the bedroom, shall I?" I ask after a moment.

"It belongs in the bedroom, on the chest of drawers," he says quietly, holding it out. I feel like a right wanker as I take it back; I've obviously upset him. I head for the stairs. How the fuck does Edward get up these stairs?

"Yes, Lucy was very beautiful," he says. "I always said that if we had children they better have her looks not mine. It was her eyes and smile. She had one of those smiles, you know."

I sit down on the sofa opposite him.

Edward's wife was sick for years. He took care of her here in the house until she died six years ago. They never had children.

I listen to Edward for a while. He tells me the same stories a couple of times and I look at the photograph and try to imagine the woman that it shows as a person in the world.

When he has finished, Edward pauses and then, with some disapproval, says "You didn't drink your coffee!" He gestures accusingly towards the evidence.

"Edward," I say, laughing "This is terrible, terrible coffee. When I go shopping let me get you something that tastes like it has actually seen a coffee bean at some point."

Edward has developed a taste for the supermarket's own value coffee and will not be persuaded to invest in a superior option. I try to count out the money in front of him, "Look Edward, I'm taking one hundred pounds, ten, twenty," but he just waves me away.

It takes me maybe a couple of hours or so to drop the clothes off at the laundrette, get around the supermarket and pick the clothes up again afterwards. I go through all of my purchases with Edward when I get back, and although he does not approve of all of them – he is particularly perplexed at my insistence that he should occasionally spray something called Fabreeze around the house – on the whole he watches with delight as I produce endless specimens of his favourite brands and products from plastic bags. We line up tins of soup and beans in the cupboard and we put the fruit in a bowl in the middle of the living room. We divide large value packs of mince and chicken into small individual portions and we freeze them.

I put Edward's clothes back in the wardrobes and I get the toiletries into the bathroom cabinet. When he is not looking I hide the jar of Peruvian medium-roast behind the kettle.

I try to show Edward the receipt and count the change out with him but he waves me away again, stubborn sod that he is. There is a pound missing, Edward, I say – because I had to use a supermarket trolley to get everything back. He opens a drawer in the living room to reveal a hoard of banknotes and drops the change in.

"You have to be much more careful with your money, Edward," I tell him, "You can't just walk around with handfuls of cash stuffed in your pockets."

"Yes I must go to the bank and speak with Peter," he says, "I always deal with Peter."

"Peter has retired, Edward," I say "He doesn't work at the bank anymore. There's a girl called Gemma, though. You can ask for her. Gemma is a good one, she's okay. Gemma-with-a-G."

"Gemma," he says "Yes, okay, I shall see if I can deal with her. Gemma-with-a-G."

Edward says thank you only once, and does so with such sincerity that he gets all teary-eyed, the silly bastard. I tell him that I'll drop in some time for a cup of coffee. As I'm leaving he pushes a twenty pound note at me. He refuses to hear my protests, and as he rubs at his eyes I think it best not to voice them. With a quick wave he shuts the door behind me.

I light a pre-rolled rolly and I walk around Edward's darkening, deserted street, which has seen better days and which offers no cross-section of society. After a few minutes I make sure that Edward isn't at the window and I push the twenty through the letterbox.

On my way home I spot an ATM and decide to try my luck – without hesitation it yields two crisp ten-pound notes. You're okay, Gemma-with-a-G – you're a good one.

.

# Auguries of Experience

## *Annabel Banks*

Once she is properly covered over we rub mud from shovels and head back to the beach. The waist-length grass is hard to wade through and I stumble, but don't complain. Neither of the boys speak to me. Carrying Lisa had been difficult; the purple curtain unfolding, her arms hanging down, half-closed fists dragging across the sand as if she were trying to slow our progress towards the cherry-tree meadow. We rested by one of the burnt cottages, laying Lisa as gently as we could on the ground, and Phil looked over the blackened fence into the garden.

"It's pretty, Jen."

"No." I wiped the sweat from my face with my sleeve. "We promised." But I knew they were thinking that between crying and being sick she hadn't known what she was saying.

It wasn't really about her, though.

At least the way back is easier. We climb through scrubby dunes, careful to avoid the traps of metal and wood that lay entwined in the deeper hollows. A tiny scratch is a serious injury now; we watch each other's health, for coughs, for nosebleeds. I think of broken bones the way I used to think about bullet wounds. We brush our teeth carefully. We never run. Ahead of me the boys break through the line of tangled shrubs to step onto the shore, and I watch the sand glitter as it shifts under their thick-soled boots. Phil turns to see where I am. I raise my hand and he nods, turning to slip an arm around Sam's shoulders.

I crunch my slow way over the sand. The glass is everywhere now: shining specks collect in eye-corners and belly buttons, jagged mirrors sit in the branches of trees to be shaken out by the wind. Every time I drink I feel tiny cuts on my lips and tongue and imagine all the glass I've swallowed embedded in my stomach wall, like diamonds in a coal face. I know it can't reach my heart, but I feel it there, all the same: brittle and desperate and cold.

Lisa hated the sharpness of this new world. She told me the shoreline was a battle that the sea would win, edges tumbled smooth by the steady wash of the ocean and the years she didn't have.

"I can see it," she said, eyes closed. "No sand. Just round, white stones. Like pebbles in a fish tank."

"That makes us the fish, then," I said, and blew out my cheeks, making them and my eyes as round as possible. Lisa held my fingers and laughed until she coughed, lips as bright and wet as the day we found the meadow and crammed cherries into each other's smiling mouths.

It takes about twenty minutes to get home. The stone building is still whole, crouching in the bottom of a low valley where it shelters us from the wind. The plastic containers lined up on the floor are almost full of oily water and I pour some off into jars, stacking them in the cupboard that used to be a fridge. Taking the rest into the bathroom I splash my face over the dry sink, not looking in the mirror. Instead, I follow the pattern of mould that curves across the tiles like green graffiti. I'll clean that soon, I think.  And smile.

When we first found the house we had so many plans. The four of us slept for weeks, curled up together under the pile of rugs and curtains salvaged from different rooms, taking turns to creep down to the ruined kitchen, rummaging for food. We ate with our toes touching, whispering about emerging from our fabric chrysalis and doing noisy things. Phil wanted to fix the roof, build an extension, dig holes and bang hammers. I would plant flowers as well as potatoes, making up songs at the top of my voice. Lisa wanted chickens; we were going to call the hens all the same name, though we could never agree which one. They would fuss around the garden all day and be locked in a coop at night, protected from imagined foxes. Sam spoke of a boat, of rods and nets and the smell of fresh fish grilling over a fire.

"Is that safe?" Lisa rolled over and sat up, pushing her tangled hair from her face. "The fish, I mean."

Phil and I looked at each other, and it grew quiet until Sam pushed his half-eaten tin of butter beans into her hand. "If the sea's poisoned then we're fucked anyway." He gave her a wink. "Eat up."

"Yes, dad," she said, then stopped laughing and put a hand over her mouth. He hugged her, pulling her into his arms, squashing her against his filthy jumper. She was still a child, really; had been on holiday with her parents, had watched their ashes spiral up into an orange and blue cloud. "Held my breath," she told us, gathering the blanket over her face. "Didn't want to breathe them in."

I said something consoling, something about not crying. She raised her head and looked at me with dry eyes.


The boys have kicked their boots off and gone upstairs. I follow and sit cross-legged, back against the cracked plaster, on the floor because we burnt the furniture. Phil opens the bottle of vodka found on his last scavenge to the village, swigs, and hands it to me. It tastes like chemical tears. I choke on the third swallow and wipe my mouth as Sam picks up a dented tin of peaches from the food pile.

"Mixer?"

"Better save them." Phil takes the bottle again. He picks the foil from the label and uses it to clean the mud from under his nails. I like the way he keeps himself clean. Sometimes he kneels in the sea, rubbing himself with hard soap, covering his face and hair with a mass of white froth. I watch, but don't join him: I still worry about the water.

We sit in the bare room, passing the bottle between us. The sun comes through the empty window. It makes an orange square on the floor and we position ourselves as if it's a fire, shifting knees and toes around the edges. The wooden floor warms beneath us; the vodka burns my throat and blurs my vision. I shuffle nearer to Phil. He puts a hand on my shin, thumb slowly circling, and all three of us watch the glass motes dancing though the light.

Later, I stand on the sharpened sand, naked except for my boots. The summer is working its magic on my sore skin, fading burns, smoothing scars. Running a hand over my stomach I watch the orange sky boil to dregs of purple and grey; ash and dust and glass refracting the light, pouring it through the clouds as if a rainbow had exploded. The others hate it, but I come every night, holding the colours in my eyes as they seep into the horizon.

The sea keeps up its low murmuring, and I hum along as I pick my way back through the shadows. Crossing a ridge I nearly walk into the seal. It is huge, like a boulder on the black sand. Its whiskers shiver but it doesn't open its eyes. The colony is further down the shore, where the sand retreats and the plateau of grey rock rises to meet the cliff. When I watch the waves in the daytime I see sleek heads bobbing between swells but have never known one to sleep this far from the others. I hesitate, wondering if it is injured, if I should touch it, but the wind has picked up. I need to get back to the house, to put clothes on, but there is something about this creature lying so stubbornly on the razor-sharp ground. The tips of my boots gouge the sand as I lean forward, and it raises its head. I had expected a soft brown eye, like a dog's, but this is a pool of oil, an inkwell, a hole. There is nothing in the look that I can pretend to understand.

Before, I'd worked in the pub. The Sunday shift was always slow, hours full of dead minutes dragging their way towards four o'clock.

136

Dave and I poured a few cokes, cooked a few chips, and did the crossword from the back of his paper. The questions were surprisingly hard; we never managed to finish it, and every week we said we'd buy it the next day, just to fill in those answers tingling at the tip of our minds. We never did. Crosswords had been a Sunday thing, symbolising a different pace, a relaxed attitude towards cigarette breaks and text messages. A Monday thing would have had rules; Dave saying "Don't let the punters see you," instead of nudging me and muttering "Ask about six across". Separated by intent, it would have been wrong to remember, so we chose to forget.

But Monday's paper was there if I wanted it. I could have scrawled over the pages, written in the margins, filled the whole paper with ideas and answers. I could communicate with someone far away, and asked about igneous rocks, archipelagos, and the properties of glass.

Walking in, I pin blankets to the shattered window frame. Phil and Sam are sitting together on the kitchen floor watching me, and as I dress I tell them about the seal.

"Might have been driven from the colony." Sam is now building up the fire, the damp wood smoking as he lays it on the edge of the hearth to dry. I see woodlice curl into balls like tiny grey oranges, drop and roll on the cracked terracotta.

"Why?" I'm cold, despite the fire, and pull my hood up, tying the strings beneath my chin, tucking my dirty hair underneath it. "What had he done?"

"Nothing." Sam opens tins of soup and sets them on the mesh over the fire. "That's just the way it goes."

Phil opens the peaches. "We should kill it." He stabs the air with the tin opener. "Fresh meat."

Sam rubs at his face, leaving a sooty smear across his cheek. "Could you do that?"

"Maybe." Phil tips the peaches into a bowl, licks his fingers and grins at him. "Give it one of your stews. That'll finish it off."

We laugh, and Phil and I go out to fetch more wood. When we

come back Sam is kneeling in front of the bubbling tins. His tears have streaked the soot on his face "So stupid," he says. "I opened four."

Phil takes him in his arms, holding him close; Sam kisses him on the lips. They stand, wrapped around each other, and I watch them as I drink my stale water, glass twisting inside me. Sam reaches out and touches my wrist, but I pull away and bend to stir the soup.

After Sam has gone upstairs we lie in the kitchen. It's late, and the waves are loud through walls and blankets. Phil touches my back and I turn, knowing he wants me to love him again, and I do. As our heartbeats slow he lies over me, still inside me, and we share, for safety's sake. Even so, we have rules. No explanations. No naming the dead.

He begins. "Ice-cubes."

"Weather forecasts."

He shifts, and I felt the shape of his mouth on my breast. "Software."

"Breakfast radio."

He sighs, and I remember Sam trying the radio again that morning, filling the house with a hissing absence of voice. Unwilling to leave that thought in his head I take another turn.

"Children."

He looks up. I can see the firelight in his eyes.

It's been raining. I don't like to stand in the rain; like the sea, I don't trust it. But I risk the beach in an overcoat to salute the light out of the sky. Walking back in the gloom I think about seals, about how I find more now,  lying as if dead in the dunes, one black eye rolling to keep me in view; small sounds from bushes, black dots on the sea. I think about them heaving themselves up out of the water and basking on the rocks, thick skin solid and warm against the barnacled surface, and what it must be like to be driven away.

138

When I get back the house is in darkness. I find Phil and Sam curled up together in the long room, their clothes piled on the floor, one of the pink blankets tangled between their legs. They are asleep, Sam's mouth at the back of Phil's neck, and I am careful to be quiet as I pick up the water bottle and leave.

Standing at the back door I look up at the wide indigo sky. The stars come earlier now the nights are so dark; sometimes I trace a satellite's lonely path, wondering how long it will be before despair makes it a shooting star. When I put on the pan to boil water the lid clatters, and I hear the low murmur of their voices. Sam comes downstairs as I'm peeling potatoes, and when I don't move he silently bends and kisses me, lips soft against my cheek. Phil is behind him: I feel his breath on my neck as he stoops to copy Sam's gesture. They both look at me, eyes dark as seals, and I feel a shift inside my chest, something sharp drawn out and discarded. Putting the knife down, I reach out for their hands and pull them to me in the shadowy firelight.

# Peeing with Brian Greene

## *Joshua Rosaler*

After class one evening, I wondered what to do as I entered the men's room to find my professor and idol, the world-renowned physicist Brian Greene, postured confidently before one of the two adjacent urinals located against the far wall. I debated whether to take the empty spot beside him or to use one of the private toilet stalls. The first option held the potential for embarrassing and permanently traumatic mishaps. The second, however, seemed equally unattractive: by ceding the open urinal, I would be allowing my professor's authority to creep beyond the classroom into places where until now I had shat and peed with relative abandon.

I searched for a precedent to inform my decision, and remembered one afternoon two years earlier when my college roommate's friend Rawlee encountered Macaulay Culkin in the bathroom of a restaurant in Soho. Among the six free urinals, Rawlee chose the one directly adjacent to the former child star, who kept his head down in a failed effort to remain unnoticed. Rawlee stared dumbly at his celebrity neighbour, bereft of self-awareness, as the sound of their streams hitting the urinal cakes merged with almost symphonic harmony. "You're Macaulay Culkin," he stated, unblinking, as though the person he was speaking to didn't already know. Culkin avoided eye contact, but humored his admirer with a "nice to meet you" as he rushed to finish up. Culkin zipped his fly, and Rawlee switched to using his left hand so that he could offer his right one for a shake.

Ever the good sport, Culkin reluctantly indulged before washing his hands and heading back to his table.

I decided that like Rawlee, I would refuse to be intimidated by those who were more famous or successful than I was. It was true that Greene still didn't know my name after I had been raising my hand every chance I got for six months in a class of only ten or so graduate students. But now I would finally prove to myself and to my professor that I was an audacious, independent thinker who had the capacity to challenge deeply ingrained dogma and traditional hierarchies. He would admire me for my moxy and recognize my potential for greatness. Reverence is a petty emotion, I told myself, not entirely convinced, as I made my way sheepishly up to the porcelain receptacle.

*Seven years earlier, February 1999.* One weekend during my sophomore year of high school, my father called me in to the living room to watch Charlie Rose. The guest was Greene, who looked barely thirty and was a newly tenured theoretical physicist and mathematician at Columbia. I had first heard of Greene a couple of weeks earlier when my father gave me a long feature article about him and his research on string theory that he had come across in New York Magazine, thinking it might appeal to me because of my long-standing interest in physics. The article, titled *He's Got the World on a String*, began opposite a full page head shot of Greene's handsome, contemplative gaze, and contained stories about Greene solving equations in his head while bored at a cocktail party, or working as a consultant on quantum chromodynamics for John Lithgow's role as a zany physics professor on *Third Rock from The Sun*, or proving advanced theorems in algebraic geometry only minutes out of the womb. It was full of fawning quotes from colleagues, such as, "He's a great communicator, he's charismatic, he's clearly top-of-the-heap intellectually. So the fact that he has gobs of raw physical appeal on top of that — it gives him a really serious mystique." *This person is better than you in every conceivable respect*, seemed to be the author's main point. *He's even funnier and more down to earth than you are.* Nevertheless, it impressed me deeply that the lame anecdotes and bland sycophancy for once were being conjured to build the mystique not of an actor or a writer or director or an artist, but of a physicist.

Greene had just authored his first book, *The Elegant Universe*, which communicated the exciting breakthroughs of contemporary theoretical physics to a general audience with eloquence, flair and clarity unprecedented in popular physics and was receiving unanimously high praise from reviewers. Charlie Rose introduced his guest: "There is in this world a quest for the ultimate theory. Ever since Isaac Newton discovered that falling apples are pulled by gravity, physicists have been trying to find unity in Nature. Einstein made progress with his theory of relativity, but it is string theory that today comes closest to resolving the question. It is Brian Greene who comes closest to explaining string theory. He is one of the bright lights of American physics, a popular professor of physics and mathematics at Columbia. He is one of the top three string theorists of his generation. He is also an occasional actor, a Harvard graduate and a Rhodes Scholar." As my father and I watched Greene seduce Rose and his audience with poetic ruminations on the symphony of the cosmos, it occurred to me, as it did to my father, that the kind of life that Greene had made for himself – a life apparently full of purpose, recognition and material comfort – might be something worth aspiring to.


*Four years later, March 2003.* It is three fifteen in the afternoon, and I have just woken up. I am passing winter break of my sophomore year at Harvard at my father's house in Connecticut, where I have fallen into my natural routine of going to bed at 5 and waking up at 3, showering sporadically, and dividing my waking hours between physics problem sets, television, and naps. I enter my father's bedroom, where he is lying down, working in bed, to give him a good morning kiss on the head before I cross the hall to take my morning shit. As I settle comfortably into my seat, I find that here, in my father's most recent issue of *Esquire* (which he has subscribed to only so that he can follow the budding career of a family friend my age who has an internship at the magazine), appearing in a Style Section feature titled *The Meaning of Life Meets Winter Style*, is none other than Greene, dapper as ever, posed before a starry background with a caption beneath that reads: "The questions we're trying to address with string theory are the ones that, in one form or another, our species has grappled with for thousands of years. How is it that we're here? How will it all end? If we can gain some insight, we're ultimately getting a clearer sense of how we fit into the universe. We've yet to get there, but that's the goal. Wool overcoat ($1,980) by Etro; cashmere blazer ($3,905) by Brunello Cucinelli; cotton-linen shirt ($95) by Pure DKNY."

How do you make physics sexy? You dress it in eternal, profoundly philosophical terms and a $4,000 sport coat.

*Two years later, June 2005.* Shortly before graduation, I was climbing the stairs of Harvard's experimental particle physics building to find Andy, the young assistant professor, exhausted new father, and once bright-eyed but now world-weary academic who had supervised my senior research project. I wanted to let him know I'd been accepted into a masters program at Columbia and to thank him again for his recommendation. I hadn't been very fond of the research he'd given me to do, which consisted mostly of writing computer code, or fit in very well with the rest of the research group, but Andy had been patient, supportive and generous with his advice and I was grateful.

I took a circuitous route up to the third floor to avoid a potential run-in with Melissa, the leader of the group, who had sent me out of a recent meeting with my tail between my legs. I'd come into the meeting late, and as usual, hadn't understood a word, though I did my poor best to look engaged. Near the end, she asked if anyone had a pen. Eager to finally contribute, I rushed to get one from my bag and handed it to her. "We knew there was a reason you were here," she said as she grabbed the pen from me.

I found Andy at one of the desks working on his laptop.

"Hey Andy." He looked up from the screen.

"I just wanted to let you know I got into Columbia, and to thank you again for everything. I've really appreciated all of your help."

Pausing to stare out the window behind me, he finally replied, "Well, I guess you'll finally get to see Brian Greene in the flesh," and then returned to his work.


I tried to buy myself some time in the hope that Greene would finish before I started. But there was only so long I could spend unzipping, pushing aside the flaps of my coat and fleece, and pretending to adjust my footing before I began to arouse the suspicion of my neighbor. My five to ten second grace period passed quickly. As I stood there, panicking before the silent urinal, the knowledge that I had nothing to fear but fear itself was of absolutely no comfort.

For what seemed like an eternity, we stood side by side at eye level, until Greene finally rushed to give himself a shake and a zip, let out an exasperated sigh, and bolted through the swinging door with a rigid arm to clear his way. He didn't even stop to wash his hands.

After I finished, I turned to look at my expressionless, twenty-two-year-old face in the mirror, and then down at the bulky brown leather Kenneth Coles that my mother had bought for me, which I initially thought I liked, but which I now found cheap and unattractive, then made my way out of the Mathematics building to catch the next subway train to my SAT tutoring session.


After tutoring, I took the 2 train down to Emily's apartment in Park Slope. Emily and I had dated for three years in college, but since graduation, I had decided that we should shed the label of boyfriend and girlfriend and try be more like Sartre and de Beauvoir. She laughed uneasily when she told me that I wasn't the first boyfriend to suggest the pair of commitment-phobic philosophers as a model for the relationship.

She opened the door to find me in anguish on the stoop.

"Buddy, what happened?"

"I don't want to talk about it."

"Did something happen in Brian Greene's class?"

"Yeah," I said, collapsing onto her bed, burying my face in her pillow. I needed to unburden myself, but shuddered at the notion of adding this particular bit of ammunition to her arsenal of blackmail material. I resolved not to give her any more information.

"Oh no. What was it?"

I refused to speak. "WHAT?!" she cried, stomping her foot on the hardwood floor. "Come on buddy, you can't not tell me."

I remained motionless, resolving that my secret would go with me to the grave – as long as Greene kept his mouth shut. I panicked and grew short of breath as I imagined Greene recounting the incident to the faculty and the other grad students. I dreaded confronting an entire physics department that judged me for having the hubris to pee next to Brian Greene.

Without looking up from my pillow, I was able to envision the expression of intense concentration on Emily's face as her brain made optimal use of everything she had learned about me over the previous three years to hone in on the single correct answer: brow furrowed into a deep crease at the center of her forehead, mouth slack, large, frog-like green eyes fixed intently at a spot on the floor.

"Did you say something stupid in class?" she said, turning to me for confirmation.

I shook my head, to clarify that of course it wasn't my brains I was worried about.

"Did something happen in the bathroom?"

No response.

"You couldn't pee in front of him?"

Again, no response.

"Aw, that's really embarrassing buddy ... he probably thinks you're a huge homo." She was punishing me for not coming clean. "So what are you gonna do the next time you see him? .... Do you think you'll keep going to class? ... Do you think he'll tell anyone?"

Emily, who aspired to be a poet and novelist like her parents, relished in collecting and recounting humiliating stories from her friends in order to entertain her other friends. "Actually, I kind of wish it had happened to me," she said, for the moment attempting to console me with her usual rationalisation: that it was possible to come to terms with anything as long as it could be used as material.

We passed a lazy Friday evening in Emily's quiet, unlit room as I mourned the death of my dreams, bore her mockery, and wondered how I would ever make the world appreciate the unique depths of my turmoil.

## Patti Smith

is a poet, rock musician, activist and artist. Her latest book of poetry, *Auguries of Innocence,* is out now.

---

## Annabel Banks

studies English Literature at Lucy Cavendish College, Cambridge. She has had poetry published in the smaller magazines, writes dramas and short stories, and is busy plotting her first novel.

## Tiffany Bergin

is doing a PhD in criminology at Queens' College, Cambridge. Her research focuses on criminological policy diffusion and quantitative methods. She was born in Hong Kong and grew up in the United States.

## Jesse Bordwin

studies English, at Wadham College, Oxford. Born in an earthquake and raised by wolves, he is finally becoming what he's always wanted to be: an unrepentant writer and unabashed New Yorker with a wiry beard and open arms.

## Patrick Kingsley

studies English at Emmanuel College, Cambridge. He likes typography and cricket. He lives in London.

## Charlotte Geater

studies English at St Edmund College, Oxford. She was a Foyle Young Poet three years in a row, and is on the editorial team for the online magazine *Pomegranate*.

## Alashiya Gordes

studies English at Newnham College, Cambridge. She loves playing with words, both on the page and on stage, and writes with an ear to reading aloud - to see what happens when words dare the air.

### Fibian Kavulani Lukalo
is doing a PhD in the Sociology of Education at Newnham College, Cambridge. Listening to the sounds made by children, the stories their daily lives reveal and appreciating the manner in which they reveal their joy and pain is something she desires to make time for always. In turn, sharing their experiences through words is her gift to these children.

### Elizabeth MacNeal
studies English at Somerville College, Oxford. She hopes to become a novelist and is in the process of writing her first novel.

### Edward Maltby
studies French and German at St John's College, Cambridge. He is from Sheffield. He likes Appolinaire, Bruce Springsteen and socialism; he can be reached at *edward.maltby@googlemail.com*.

### Laura Marsh
studies English at Christ Church, Oxford. She has twice been a winner of the Foyle Young Poets of the Year Award, in 2005 and 2006, and was a winner of the Rialto Young Poets competition and a Christopher Tower Poetry Prize in 2007. Her work appeared in the *Rialto*, *Acumen* and *Pomegranate*.

### Pablo Navarro MacLochlainn
no longer studies History of Art at King's College, Cambridge. He, he walk like this cuz he can back it up.

### Richard O'Brien
studies English and French at Brasenose College, Oxford. He is a member of the editorial team of the *Pomegranate* poetry ezine and his first pamphlet was published in July 2009 on tall-lighthouse press.

### Marcelle Olivier
is completing doctoral research at Keble College, Oxford. She grew up in South Africa. She has published intermittently over the last ten years but

is currently working on a collection of poetry inspired by the conflicting themes inherent in archaeology. This is her third consecutive appearance in the Mays.

## Michael Perfect

is doing a PhD focussing on representations of racism and multiculturalism in contemporary British fiction at Clare Hall, Cambridge. He is from Manchester and studied at the University of East Anglia and the University of Nottingham before coming to Cambridge. He works tirelessly on both his PhD and his novel except for when he finds better things to do.

## Johnny Regan

studies Romanticism and Versification at Wolfson College, Cambridge. He is from Glasgow. He has been published in the *Times Literary Supplement*, *The British Association for Romantic Studies and Women: A Cultural Review*.

## Ashley Riches

studies English at King's College, Cambridge. He likes writing and music. Next year, he is going to the Guildhall School of Music in London.

## Lizzie Robinson

studies Classics at Queens' College, Cambridge.

## Joshua Rosaler

is doing a DPhil in Philosophy at Pembroke College, Oxford. Among other things, he enjoys writing about scientists and their ideas from a literary perspective, and draws inspiration from his time studying physics. At Oxford, he investigates problems concerning the philosophical justification of science as a path to objective knowledge as well as more specific issues in the conceptual foundations of modern physics. He has always had a strong interest in journalism and creative writing.

## Miguel Santa Clara

studies Architecture at King's College, Cambridge. He feels blind walking through a city without a camera. He ignores stagnant icons, finding interest in the constant transformation of the city by the anonymous individual.

## Colette Sensier

studies English at King's College, Cambridge. She is originally from Sussex. She has won several young person's poetry competitions and has been published in magazines including the Rialto.

## Merlin Sheldrake

studies Natural Sciences at Clare College, Cambridge. He took up doodling in nursery school and remains a keen practitioner to this day.

## Dylan Spencer-Davidson

studies French and German Literature at Queens' College, Cambridge.

## Molly Stern

studies English and Modern Languages at Wadham College, Oxford. She is a California-born cake enthusiast with a fondness for deep-sea animals and abnormal medical conditions. She spends her day in solitary confinement studying German, Old English, and Japanese literature.

## David Story

studies English at Homerton College, Cambridge. He is a resident of London and the world. He is a connoisseur of magazines and alternative grain breads; sometimes together.

## Emily Tesh

studies Classics at Trinity College, Cambridge. She is one of the two editors-in-chief of the *Pomegranate* poetry zine (www.pomegranate.me.uk) and her poetry has appeared in *Magma* and *Mimesis* magazines, won the

Foyle Young Poets of the Year award, and been shortlisted for the Stephen Spender prize for verse translation. She finds it incredibly difficult to keep short stories short.

## *Anna Trench*
studies English at King's College, Cambridge.

## *Micah Trippe*
is doing a PhD in the Department of Architecture. He is a member of King's College and a New Yorker.